DEAD STRANGE

First published in North American 2012 by Zest Books
35 Stillman Street, Suite 121, San Francisco, CA 94107
www.zestbooks.net
Created and produced by Zest Books, San Francisco, CA

Typeset in Egyptienne, Trade Gothic, and Toronto Gothic

Teen Nonfiction / History / Arts & Entertainment

Library of Congress Control Number: 2012933458

ISBN: 978-1-936976-27-0

CREDITS
BOOK EDITORS: Dan Harmon and Mariah Gumpert
CREATIVE DIRECTOR: Hallie Warshaw
ART DIRECTOR/COVER DESIGN: Tanya Napier
GRAPHIC DESIGN: Marissa Feind
MANAGING EDITOR: Pam McElroy
PRODUCTION EDITOR: Keith Synder
EDITORIAL ASSISTANT: Ann Edwards

TEEN ADVISORS: Amelia Alvarez, Ema Barnes, Anna Livia Chen,
Huitzi Herrera-Sobal, and Felicity Massa

Manufactured in China
SCP 10 9 8 7 6 5 4 3 2 1
4500361570

First published in Great Britain 2003
© 2003 by Arcturus Publishing Limited
Arcturus Publishing Limited
26/27 Bickels Yard
151-153 Bermondsey Street
London, SE1 3HA
UNITED KINGDOM

All cover photos and interior photos pgs. 45, 131, and 135 courtesy of iStockphoto.

DEAD STRANGE

the bizarre truths behind
50 world-famous mysteries

matt Lamy

INtRODUCtION

Have you ever had the feeling that there's more to our world than meets the eye? That some things happen for which there just isn't any logical explanation? Or that the dividing line between waking life and dreams (not to mention nightmares) isn't as clear as we might think? Well, you're not alone.

Humans have always sought answers for the unexplained, but even when we do find answers it often seems like we only wind up with… more questions! Through advances in science and technology we often come up with better questions than we had before, but, at the same time, some questions never change. Where did we come from? What happens to us after we die? Why is there evil in the world? What was that sound we just heard? And who was Jack the Ripper, really!?

Zombies, voodoo, Bigfoot, the lost city of El Dorado, the magic of Ouija boards, and the idea of angels and reincarnation, are all, in their way, attempts to address these big questions (or, potentially, ways for these questions to begin addressing us). These mysterious phenomena have been an essential part of every human culture. In the Northwestern United States people still hunt for evidence of Bigfoot; the Loch Ness Monster has been eluding boaters in Scotland for centuries; vampires and zombies fascinate audiences all over the world; and kids everywhere still try to make contact with the dead via their families' Ouija boards.

In this book, you'll learn about all kinds of seemingly unexplainable phenomena. Some of these seem to lie forever just beyond our grasp (like Bigfoot pictures, which are always blurry, or Jack the Ripper's true identity, which constantly eludes us.) Some tales have been researched and disproved countless times, and yet people still cling to them. And others seem unlikely to ever be solved. But who knows, some of these mysteries could be solved tomorrow! After all, it seems like we finally figured out what happened to Anastasia. Maybe we'll have similar luck with the Big Bang or the Holy Grail!

Keeping an open mind to the possibility that there's more to this world than we can test and measure seems like a pretty good idea—and it definitely makes life a lot more exciting. And you never know—with an open mind and a watchful eye you just might discover the next unexplained mystery yourself!

DEAD 5TRANGE:

the BIZARRE tRUTHS BEHIND 50 WORLD-famous mysteries

► ALCHEMY ◄

Scientists believe that the discovery of oxygen in the eighteenth century led to the birth of chemistry as we know it. Before that, many cultures had examined the properties of different materials without ever forming a coherent theory to link their qualities. These ancient studies were known as alchemy or transmutation. Scientists once believed that metals underwent a profound change as they oxidized, and these scientists hoped that the ultimate transmutation process would turn common metals into gold or silver. Alchemy was the name that was given to the idea of making gold from scratch. Modern chemistry has proven such a theory to be completely impossible, but for thousands of years it was thought to be true.

Many of the world's greatest minds believed in the possibility of making gold from base ingredients. In fact, it was such a widely held belief that King Henry IV of England encouraged all intelligent men in the country to study the subject so that the nation's great debts could be paid. And in later years, many other rulers also supported alchemists and their experiments. Others feared the repercussions of transmutation, and in the second century BCE China actually made the production of gold by alchemy an offense punishable by death, while the Roman Emperor Diocletian ordered the destruction of all Egyptian texts that advocated alchemical procedures.

Diocletian and the Chinese authorities were wise to be wary, for the ancient Egyptian and Far Eastern peoples were then the world's authorities on alchemy. Some still revere mystical Eastern alchemical practices to this day, and the Egyptians are said to have spread their knowledge on to other peoples, particularly in the Arab world, where

PEOPLE ARE STILL DOING THIS?

Alchemy is still practiced today, though most people (we hope!) are no longer trying to turn metal into gold. Today's practitioners are trying to find healing remedies, and using alchemical symbols as part of spiritual practices such as Kabbalah. Instead of trying to achieve eternal youth (like ancient alchemists in the East), they believe in being connected to the universe. Some of them believe that alchemy's principles can help improve modern science, especially in the study of cloning and DNA. Some even believe that alchemy can lead to time travel.

Alchemists hard at work, trying to turn base metals into gold (with the aid of smoke, chamber pots, plungers, and a cast of thousands).

the seventh-century ruler King Khalid was said to be a master of the subject. Indeed, the word *alchemy* is thought to have been derived from the Arabic word for Egyptian art, *al-khem*. In the following centuries it is said that the Sufi Islamic movement used alchemy as part of its religious teachings.

Alchemy has always had strong religious connections. Albertus Magnus and St. Thomas Aquinas were both experts on the subject. Aquinas even wrote a text asking if it was ethically correct to pass off gold created by alchemy as real gold. Another holy man, the fourteenth-century pontiff Pope John XXII, wrote a major work on the subject, and also wrote a great text damning fraudulent alchemists. When he died in 1334, he left behind large amounts of wealth, leading some to speculate that it had been created through alchemy. Even Martin Luther may have believed that alchemy was beneficial for affirming Church doctrines. Scientists Sir Isaac Newton and Robert Boyle were also sympathetic to alchemy.

Modern chemistry has proven that the alchemists' goals were impossible, but our knowledge still grows in strange ways. The realm of unstable radioactive materials and the achievement of scientific transmutation through nuclear reactions have opened new avenues of thought. Another goal of alchemy was to find the elixir of life that would cure all ills and keep people young for eternity. Again, although modern science has dismissed these methods, experiments in the fields of DNA and cloning suggest that this idea is not too far removed from reality.

Other offshoots of this medical branch of alchemy are also considered valid by some people in our modern age. Homeopathy and aromatherapy, for example, are direct descendants of old alchemy studies, and acupuncture and hypnosis are also derived from alchemical work. Some modern alchemists still believe, however, that imbalances in the body cause illnesses, and many in the medical profession regard these people as "quacks." The subject has also been linked with many New Age ideas and theories, which has not helped the public accept it as a genuine and serious area of interest. Many people continue to practice alchemy and maintain that it is a valid subject. Science tends to disagree, but our development and view of the world still owes a lot to this ancient art.

ALIEN ABDUCTIONS

Aliens are said to erase the minds of their victims, so what actually happens during an abduction is often only revealed through regressive hypnosis or piecing together known facts. However, most abduction stories follow broadly similar lines. Generally, the person being abducted feels compelled, or is forced, to go into an alien spacecraft where he or she encounters the visitors. These are often described as being small, gray figures with large black eyes and hairless bodies. They are frequently reported as having large skulls, and they communicate with their human captive using telepathy, telling the person not to be scared, that they will not be harmed.

The candidate is usually scanned or examined, and then placed on an operating table. This part of the abduction is often a blur, even during hypnosis, but it seems the aliens perform a series of tests, including extensive sexual experiments. They prod, probe, and manipulate the abductee's body. Some abductees even report having tracking devices or other equipment implanted under their skin.

The human is returned to wherever he or she was picked up, often remembering absolutely nothing. Consequently the person is left perplexed, as several unaccountable hours have passed. The physical effects are said to be striking. Many people are bruised all over their bodies, and suffer painful headaches the next morning. Abductees often have terrible nosebleeds and bizarre but small puncture wounds at points on their skin. Female abduction victims are particularly prone to suffering sexual pains.

A CASE IN POINT: FIRE IN THE SKY

The 1993 film *Fire in the Sky* portrays the real-life 1975 abduction of logger Travis Walton. Abducted in an Arizona forest, with his logging crew as witnesses, Walton went missing for five days. After a massive search, he reappeared, cold, weak, and hungry. His memories included lying on an examining table surrounded by bald creatures with huge heads and eyes. Still controversial, the Walton case was one of the first abduction cases to be well-documented and attract mainstream media attention.

In all cases, the victims feel an extreme sense of fatigue.

The psychological results are often even more extreme. Some people feel that they love the aliens and have been enriched by the contact. These abductees believe the visitors have come to warn us of potential harm and help mankind protect the planet. But these types of experiences are in the minority. Many victims feel a sense of violation and despair. Often, they also feel confusion, disbelief, and a sense of possible insanity. Many abduction victims need counseling to regain some sense of stability and, in cases of extreme trauma, have been known to commit suicide. However, many researchers wonder if abduction memories are themselves caused by psychological problems, rather than the reverse.

Alien abductions first entered the public consciousness in September 1961 when strange beings reportedly captured Barney and Betty Hill. The Hills gave an account under hypnosis a few years later indicating that all kinds of strange experiments had been performed on them. Betty had seen the aliens insert a probe into her belly button, and Barney claims he was forced to provide a sample of his sperm. The one incongruous detail they

This alien—who appears fairly typical looking to us humans—is actually quite the ladies' man on his home planet.

did provide was that the aliens, rather than having large black eyes, actually had "wrap-around" receptors. Skeptics point out that the Hills' testimonies were given less than two weeks after a television episode about aliens with wraparound eyes.

This factor is one that repeatedly appears in abduction stories. The descriptions of aliens and their craft are often identical to stereotypical, 1930s-style cosmic invaders. Most of the details revealed could have been derived from the imagination of a comic book writer. We also don't know of any cases where souvenirs have been brought back from an alien craft. However, there are a few examples featuring extremely disturbing physical evidence. In one case, a pregnant woman was abducted by aliens who removed her fetus. She had previously gone for an ultrasound that confirmed her unborn child was present and doing fine, but when she went to the doctor afterward, it had simply disappeared.

Another example involves people who actually found alien implants in their bodies. There is even a rumor that a private clinic in California has removed a number of strange implants from abductees' bodies. If these stories are true, there can be no denying that alien meetings leave physical scars on the victims.

The reported evidence on the bodies of abductees is hard to dismiss, and if an implant is ever officially removed and studied, it could act as conclusive proof. Until then, many people may stay skeptical, believing that this phenomenon is nothing more than the product of otherworldly imaginations.

▶ AMITYVILLE ◀

The most famous and horrific ghost story of the last century must be that of 112 Ocean Avenue, in Amityville, New York. The terrifying tale has been turned into a best-selling book, a successful film, and several sequels, and has captured the public's attention like no other haunting. Indeed, such is its place in the American consciousness that most people assume that it is a true story—and that is certainly how it was publicized. There is no doubt that some awful events did take place in the building, but were they really caused by ghostly actions?

The now-infamous three-story Dutch colonial house was built in 1924. The original owners lived happily in the building for many years, raising a family and leaving the house to their daughter, who had such fond memories of her childhood home that she moved her own family into it. In 1960 that family sold the house to a couple who lived there until their divorce in 1965.

In June 1965, the DeFeo family bought the house. They were an unhappy family, and the father, Ronald DeFeo Sr., was known to be abusive. Over a period of nine years the family did not seem to experience any type of frightening event other than those inflicted by paternal forces. That all changed, however, on the night of November 18, 1974, when one son, Ronald DeFeo Jr., shot and killed his mother, father, two brothers, and two sisters.

Just over a year later, in December 1975, a young couple bought the house. George and

A CASE IN POINT: THE ORIGINAL "MOST HAUNTED" HOUSE

Long before Amityville, one of the original "most haunted" houses in America, there was the Congelier House in Pittsburgh, Pennsylvania. In 1871, Lyda Congelier discovered that her husband, Charles, was having an affair with the maid. In anger, she stabbed her husband and decapitated the maid. A later resident, Dr. Adolph Brunrichter, murdered young women in the home. Some reported hearing a woman's sobbing and others suffered mysterious deaths in the house. In 1927, a nearby natural gas storage tank exploded, destroying the home along with several others. Was it missed? Not likely.

Kathy Lutz and Kathy's three children moved in, knowing the building's terrible history. Almost immediately they began experiencing strange phenomena. The Lutzes saw doors and windows open by themselves and heard bizarre noises. A devilish voice ordered a Catholic priest who had come to exorcise the house to get out.

Things rapidly grew worse. The Lutzes said that blood and sticky goo oozed from the walls, clouds of flies appeared on windows, ghostly hooded apparitions manifested, and one of the children started communicating with a demonic pig called Jodie. One night a supernatural force even threw Kathy Lutz from her bed, and it was famously claimed that the face of the devil appeared in the brickwork of the fireplace.

After 28 days of this horror, the Lutzes moved out. They soon went to the media with their story. In February 1976, a television news team filmed Ed and Lorainne Warren—two of America's most famous paranormal investigators—conducting séances at the house. The Warrens stated the house was indeed haunted with evil spirits, but other investigators were not convinced.

Dr. Stephen Kaplan, the executive director of the Parapsychology Institute of America,

The events at Amityville are certainly up for debate, but the fashion sense of George and Kathy Lutz is not.

based in New York, initially had great doubts about the story, and discovered some inconsistencies in what the Lutzes reported. However, his studies were ignored. It transpired that the couple had already collaborated with an author, Jay Anson, and had written a book, *The Amityville Horror: A True Story*, an instant best-seller upon its release in 1977. A successful film version was released in 1979.

As Kaplan suspected, there were some dubious actions and motives behind the Amityville tale. It was revealed that Ronald DeFeo Jr.'s defense lawyer had met with the Lutzes before their story was released. Kaplan found no evidence to support many of the claims written in their book, but he did discover that the Lutzes had returned to the house to hold a garage sale only a couple of weeks after apparently fleeing in terror. Similarly, many investigators noticed that the Lutzes had received contracts for book and film rights as soon as they decided to publicize their account.

Three different families have lived in the house since the Lutzes left, with no reports of ghostly experiences. Dr. Stephen Kaplan's in-depth report and its subsequent revelations about the house were never viewed with as much interest as the dramatic original story, but a book he wrote, *The Amityville Horror Conspiracy*, was published some years after his death. Many investigators and cynics have concluded that the whole case really revolved around money, rather than paranormal influences. It seems the evil forces in this story may have less to do with supernatural unknowns, and more with all-too-common moral failings.

► ANASTASIA/ANNA ANDERSON ◄

In February 1920, two years after the execution of the last Russian tsar, Nicholas II, and his family, a young woman attempted suicide by jumping off a bridge in Berlin. She was rescued, but when she arrived at the hospital she had no proof of identity on her and would not reveal her name. The hospital sent her to an insane asylum where she was recognized as the tsar's daughter, Grand Duchess Tatiana. The woman denied that she was Tatiana, but over time revealed that she was actually the tsar's other daughter, the Duchess Anastasia. She explained that the bayonets of the Communist death squad soldiers had been blunt and she had survived the assassination attempt. One of the soldiers who came to remove the bodies had noticed that she was still alive and spirited her away to Romania. She had come to Berlin to find her aunt, Princess Irene, but the fear of being recognized led to her take desperate measures. The woman adopted the name Anna Anderson, and spent much of her life trying to prove she was Anastasia.

When news of her appearance first spread, one of Alexandra's ladies-in-waiting visited the hospital, but Anderson kept her head covered with blankets so the woman declared her a fake. Similarly, Princess Irene met Anderson and refuted her claims, although in private it is said she was not so sure, and her son Sigismund actually declared that he thought Anderson was Anastasia. The community of European monarchies was generally undecided. The tsar's mistress, Mathilde Kschessinka, believed Anderson was the young princess, and Pierre Guillard, Anastasia's former tutor, also initially declared his support before changing his

The survivor of the massacre of the Russian royal family, or a Polish factory worker named Franziske?

mind. The family of another court employee, the monarch's doctor, Eugene Botkin, was utterly convinced of Anderson's true royal lineage, particularly since she could speak in detail about personal correspondence between the young princesses and Botkin's children.

In attitude, Anderson certainly behaved like a princess. She was said to be demanding and arrogant, and could be consumed by fits of rage. She spoke excellent English, French, and German, and could fully understand Russian although she refused to speak it. She also had scars on her body that matched her execution claims, and facial experts argued that she looked very similar to Anastasia. She had similar physical deformities to the young princess, and calligraphic experts said their handwriting was identical. Anderson was also said to have an extensive knowledge of royal affairs. She revealed that Anastasia's uncle, Grand Duke Ernst of Hesse, had secretly visited the Russian monarchy in 1916 when the two families were actually at war. This fact was only categorically proven in 1966, but Ernst always denied the claims.

It has been suggested that Ernst started circulating another theory, that Anderson was actually a Polish factory worker named Franziska Schanzkowski. People started to claim that Schanzkowski disappeared only a day before Anderson's appearance in Berlin. It was said that Anderson's scars had

Princess Anastasia before her assassination.

DID YOU KNOW...THE MYSTERY MAY HAVE BEEN SOLVED?

In 2007, amateur archaeologists discovered two sets of bone fragments, belonging to a 13–15 year-old boy and a 16–18 year-old girl. DNA testing confirmed that the bones likely belong to the last two unaccounted-for children: Alexei, and either Anastasia or her sister, Maria. Some skeptics still believe that the children could not have been Tsar Nicholas's, that eyewitness reports of the murder indicated the children's bodies were crushed to powder. But royal-watchers can rest easy in the belief that DNA analysis does not lie.

In 1991, the remains of eight people were found in Siberia. Forensic testing suggests the corpses of Nicholas, Alexandra, and three of their children were among the bodies. British scientists compared their DNA with samples of Anderson's hair, and found no match. However, Anderson did seem to have extremely similar DNA results to blood samples taken from the grand-nephew of Franziska Schanzkowski. So it appears the mystery of Anna Anderson has been put to rest. Except for one thing: when Russian authorities uncovered the royal bodies in 1991, two corpses were missing. One was the tsar's son Alexei. The other was his youngest daughter, Anastasia.

arisen from a time when Schanzkowski had dropped a live grenade while working at an armaments factory. However, Anderson was small and frail, whereas Schanzkowski was raised on a farm and supposedly had a very stocky build. Anderson continually tried to prove her heritage, but she never succeeded conclusively in a court of law. In late 1968 she married a wealthy American called John Manahan, and she died of pneumonia in 1984. Her body was cremated, but advances in DNA testing meant her death was not the end of the saga.

► ANGELS ◄

The idea of angels is not exclusive to the Roman Catholic Church. Many people of all religions have experienced feelings or events that instilled a belief that something is watching over them, protecting them. Whether that is a divine being depends on the person's own belief in God. There is also a case for saying that many people feel guided by a guardian angel, which does not have to be a religious entity, but can be a deceased relative or friend. In both cases, the angel's role is to give warning of impending danger, and comfort in times of difficulty.

CHRONOLOGY: ANGEL GUIDES

Throughout history there have been stories of angels appearing to people and affecting the outcome of major world events. Some of the biggies are:

❋ First century: The angel Gabriel appears to the Virgin Mary, saying she will be the mother of Jesus.

❋ Seventh century: The angel Gabriel appears to Mohammed, revealing the Koran.

❋ Fifteenth century: The archangel Michael tells Joan of Arc to lead the French army to victory.

❋ Nineteenth century: An angel named Moroni appears to Joseph Smith, who founded the Mormon Church.

❋ Twentieth century: An angel named Metatron appears to guitarist Carlos Santana, influencing his comeback album, Supernatural.

(Okay, not every event was major.)

One fascinating story concerns Sergei Kourdakov who, as a Russian KGB agent, was instructed not to believe deity-based faiths. Indeed, Kourdakov was in a squad purposely set up to persecute and intimidate Christian groups. On one occasion, he claims his team raided a secret Bible meeting with the task of punishing those present.

An angel busily racking up some frequent flyer miles.

Kourdakov noticed an old woman standing in the corner holding her Bible. He went over to beat her, but as he pulled his arm back to punch her, some strange presence held it behind him. He turned round but there was nobody there. Eventually, Kourdakov ended up defecting to the United States.

The religious view of angels is that they are solely God's messengers. They appear to give news of great events—for example, telling the shepherds of Christ's birth. Their role is to perform God's commands and reveal the most important truths to Man. Often they instill awe in those that see them, but they are said to exude a calm confidence. Although they appear regularly throughout both the Old and New Testaments, Bible-based religions aren't the only ones that experience the phenomenon. Many races and cultures have recorded startlingly similar accounts of meetings with mystical creatures, and they are often associated with miracles and inexplicable healing powers.

It seems unfair that the horses don't get wings, too.

► AREA 51 ◄

A military base deep in the Nevada desert is surrounded by so much official secrecy that the United States government has even refused to acknowledge it exists. The CIA built the base, and all pilots, ground crews, and staff have to retire from their original military departments and join the agency before taking residency on site. As a CIA installation it operates independently of other government departments. Signs at the entrance warn all visitors that they have no constitutional rights on site, and armed units guard the perimeter. It is the UFO world's worst-kept secret, and the area is now a pilgrimage point for alien watchers. This is Area 51.

Built in the 1950s around the Groom Lake Air Force base, and next to the Nevada atomic test range, Area 51 was a perfect site to carry out classified aircraft tests. It had a large flat surface perfect for laying runways, few local residents, and a highly unattractive reputation to new settlers due to the nearby nuclear pollution. Initially it was built purely for testing the U2 spy plane, but the program was such a success that all the United States secret aircraft were experimentally flown there. The base grew in size, creating its own small community, and the landing strip was increased to three miles long. The Blackbird and Stealth planes were developed on-site, and the base's hangar houses countless unknown technologies. Many people believe these technologies are, quite literally, from a different planet, and the base is actually a

test zone and hiding site for alien aircraft. People have reported seeing strange lights in the sky above the base at night, and many

SPOTLIGHT ON...
THE SKYLAB INCIDENT

If a place doesn't officially exist, can you take a photo of it? In 1974, astronauts on the Skylab space station inadvertently photographed the "nonexistent" Groom Lake facility, despite having specific orders not to do so. Further, the site was the only site on earth with that designation, meaning that the CIA considered it the most sensitive, secretive spot in the world. The photos, which are still classified, caused great controversy within the government, prompting the question: What the heck was in those pictures?

watchers believe the site hides enormous underground installations.

The most in-depth knowledge of Area 51 operations has come through one man, Bob Lazar, a scientist who was employed by a company called EG & G in 1989. Lazar indicated that EG & G was working on a propulsion project at its testing center near Area 51, on a base called S4. In later conversations, Lazar revealed that he and other scientists were employed to pull an alien aircraft apart and see if they could manufacture it using man-made components. As part of their work, the scientists were informed about the role of aliens in the history of the Earth, and Lazar even claims to have briefly seen, firsthand, a real, live alien at S4.

Lazar says that, over time, he decided to rebel against his employers. On the evening of March 22, 1989, he and a friend went out to the Groom Lake road and watched a flying disc test flight. The following week Lazar returned to the area with Gene Huff—a close friend of his—and several other people. They saw a disc flight, which Huff described as "the thrill of a lifetime." The disc they witnessed had a brilliant glow, and flew so close to them that they felt they had to move backward. The following week, on the way back home from another UFO-spotting trip, the group was seen and stopped by base security

patrolling the outlying area. The next day Lazar was sacked from EG & G. He has subsequently reported that nine discs are held at S4.

Some of the unsettling things that go on at the base are more "real" than others. The road to its entrance is known as "The Widow's Highway" because of the high numbers of workers at the base who die through

Examining the wreckage of either a UFO or a top-heavy weather balloon.

On site at Area 51, with either (A) six human beings, or (B) five human beings and one very human-looking alien (second from right, in all probability).

contact with fatally poisonous materials. Many experts suggest the area is a secret dumping ground for toxic substances, rather than a UFO base. In either case, the workers are sworn to secrecy, and cannot reveal details about what they have been handling to their doctors. Some of the workers' wives have launched court proceedings against the US government, which has traditionally refuted the allegations on the grounds that Area 51 does not officially exist. However, in January 2001, President Bush officially recognized the area's existence, referring to the "operating location near Groom Lake." However, Bush also said that the site was exempt from environmental disclosure requirements, so the widows are still fighting their case. But at least we now know the place is not just a figment of our imaginations.

▶ THE ARK OF THE COVENANT ◀

The Bible says that God inscribed the Ten Commandments on two stone tablets that he gave to Moses. To protect the tablets and make them portable, a wooden chest decorated with exquisite gold ornaments was built. It was about three-and-a-half feet long, just over two feet wide, and had two poles attached through gold rings on its sides. There were two carved cherubim on top, and the chest's lid was called the atonement cover or the "mercy seat." The box accompanied Moses and the Israelites on their quest for the Promised Land, and brought them victory wherever they went. When they finally founded Jerusalem, King Solomon built the Holy of Holies, or First Temple, and housed the box there. This supremely holy chest is called the Ark of the Covenant.

No single item is involved in more legends of treasure, unexplained wealth, and international intrigue than this great chest. Some legends say that the Ark was destroyed or captured by invading Egyptian forces around 925 BCE; others say that the Babylonians stole it in 586 BCE. The Jewish sect that wrote the Dead Sea Scrolls may have buried the Ark in the Jordanian desert before they were overrun. Likewise, it has been suggested that an early Christian group called the Cathars may have hidden it in an ancient church at Rennes-le-Château in France before the group was put down by the Catholic Church.

King Arthur has also been linked to the Ark's history, while many researchers claim it was taken from the Holy Land by the Knights Templar. It is said that they may have hidden it at the pit on Oak Island, or even at Rosslyn Chapel in Scotland. One theory claims that the descendants of the Knights Templar are the Freemasons, who now have the Ark under their control. In fact, many mysterious tales have also involved the Ark of the Covenant. Here, we will look at two of the most plausible theories.

Leen Ritmeyer is an archaeologist who has conducted tests on the Temple Mount in Jerusalem, and believes he has established the true position of the First Temple. He claims he has discovered a section cut out of the underlying rock that exactly matches the dimensions of the Ark. From this, Ritmeyer surmises that the Ark may be buried deep inside the Temple Mount, but it seems impossible that excavations will be carried out in the area, particularly while it continues to be the site of violent political turmoil. Many other experts also believe the Ark remains in the Holy Land, and one, an American named Ron Wyatt, even claimed to have found the sacred chest in the Garden Tomb, in the north of the old city of Jerusalem.

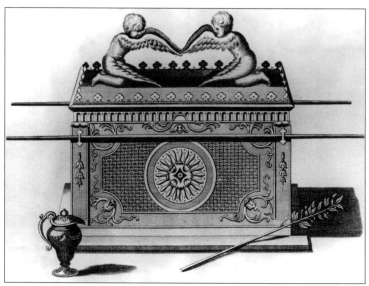

A drawing of the Ark of the Covenant. (Also included here: the less famous Pitcher of the Covenant, and the Plant of the Covenant.)

Perhaps the most celebrated theory connecting the ark with a real object revolves around eastern Africa. An Ethiopian legend claims the Queen of Sheba was impregnated by King Solomon. The child, known as Menelik, meaning "the son of the wiseman," travelled to Jerusalem when he was 20 to study in his father's court. Within a year, Solomon's priests had become jealous of the king's son and said he must return to Sheba. Solomon accepted this but said that all firstborn sons of other elders should accompany Menelik.

One of these, Azarius, was the son of Zadok, the High Priest. It was Azarius who is supposed to have stolen the Ark and taken it to Africa. Menelik then decided that their success must be divine will, and founded the "Second Jerusalem" at Aksum in Ethiopia. Today, the ancient church of St. Mary of Zion is said to house the Ark, which was traditionally brought out every January for the celebration known as Timkat.

SPOTLIGHT ON...
SOLOMON'S TEMPLE

Lost treasures of the Bible have captivated archaeologies, treasure-seekers, and conspiracy theorists for centuries. Solomon's Temple, the primary temple in ancient Jerusalem, is a prime example. The Bible describes the structure in great detail and, unlike other lost treasures, archaeologists even think they know where this one is—beneath the Temple Mount in Jerusalem. Unfortunately, excavating on the Temple Mount is practically impossible since the area is so politically sensitive. For now, archaeologists are studying similar temples that date back to the Iron Age, hoping that they are similar enough to provide some clues.

In recent years, due to the instability in the country, the Ark has been hidden away and cared for by a devoted guardian, who is the only man allowed to see the true nature of the box. Certainly, there is a lot to back this theory—for instance, Ethiopia is one of the few African countries that practices Christianity, and the national constitution ruled that the Ethiopian emperor is a direct descendant of King Solomon. Ethiopians are confident of their role in the Ark's heritage, but with so many legends vying to reveal the final resting place of the Ark of the Covenant, it is impossible to decide on one. Perhaps, as many religious groups believe, its presence will become known when the time is right.

► ATLANTIS ◄

Our knowledge of the world's most famous lost continent comes from the work of one man—Plato. The great Greek philosopher was the singular source of all information about the ill-fated island race, and while experts write long-winded theses about the age and position of Atlantis, nobody is entirely sure that Plato did not just invent the Atlantean people as an allegory for what happens when a civilization overreaches itself. Despite this, the hunt for Atlantis is as fierce as ever.

Plato lived in Greece between 428 and 348 BCE, and revealed the story of Atlantis in his dialogues *Timaeus* and *Critias*. Many of Plato's fables were fictional creations used to illustrate a point, but he repeatedly stated the history of Atlantis as fact. The dialogues recount the story of Solon, a Greek scholar who traveled to Egypt around 600 BCE to learn more about the ancient world. As Solon tried to impress his hosts with tales of Greece's achievements, the wise old Egyptian priests put him in his place. They revealed a story about a continent and a people completely unknown to him. Around 10,000 BCE, they said, a powerful race lived on an island in the west, beyond the Pillars of Hercules,

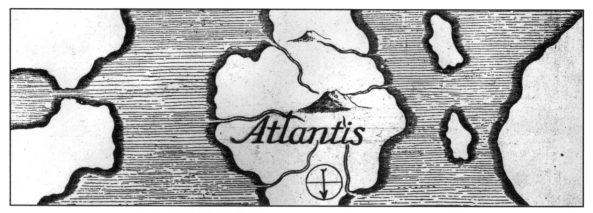

"So to get to Atlantis, just head west on the Nameless Sea, and then turn left when you hit the blobby islands."

now believed to be the land masses along the coasts of the Straits of Gibraltar. The island was the kingdom of Poseidon, the Sea God. It had a huge central mountain with a temple dedicated to the deity, and lush outlying districts. There was also an elaborate system of canals to irrigate its successful farms, and a bustling central city. The island was rich in vegetables, and home to different types of exotic animals.

The Atlanteans were originally a powerful but fair race. They were an advanced people with a prosperous trading industry, a strong and noble army, and a highly educated, cultured society. Their influence reached far and wide, and they controlled large areas of Africa, Asia, and the Mediterranean. Although the island left its inhabitants wanting for nothing, their taste for power and empire led to them overextending themselves. They failed in an attempt to conquer Athens, and retreated home to face a cataclysmic disaster. Legend says that the great god Zeus saw the corruption that had seized the island's people, and sent down upon them an immense barrage of earthquakes, fire, and water. Atlantis disappeared under the waves.

While Plato's story was well known, the renewed modern interest in Atlantis began in 1882, when a former US congressman, Ignatius Donnelly, published *Atlantis: The Antediluvian World*. Donnelly's book was a mixture of conjecture, misinterpreted fact, and actual history, but there were some interesting ideas. He noted similarities in the science and culture of native races that apparently could never have met. Likewise, the great ancient flood, which is said to have destroyed Atlantis, is logged in ancient writings and traditions of peoples around the world.

It is not known exactly who the Atlanteans were. Some say they were aliens, some

SPOTLIGHT ON...LEMURIA, THE LOST GARDEN OF EDEN

Another "lost" civilization, on the continent of Lemuria, is supposed to have existed even before Atlantis. Known as an intelligent and spiritually advanced civilization, it was reputedly destroyed by a volcano. Legends say Lemuria was the original Garden of Eden, or the birthplace of man. Influenced by Darwin's theories of evolution, people in the nineteenth century thought it was a land bridge that once connected two continents together, because lemurs had been found on both. Scientists today believe that mankind can trace its roots back to a small biological pool. So maybe it was man's birthplace after all...

believe they were descendants of the legendary Lemurians, and some say they eventually traveled west and became assimilated into Native American tribes. Similarly, the actual location of Atlantis is open to argument. Many experts suggest the island was actually in the Mediterranean, and a constant stream of archaeological investigations in the area has tried to prove this.

There are theories that Sardinia in the Mediterranean, or the island of Thera in the Aegean Sea, could be Atlantis. Both had highly evolved civilizations: the Nuraghi people on Sardinia and the Minoan culture on Thera. Both also suffered terrible natural disasters. But neither of these islands is west of the Straits of Gibraltar, so to accept them is to doubt Plato's geography. Also, the advanced races on these islands disappeared about 900 years before Plato, and he stated that Atlantis became extinct 9,000 years before him.

Other experts say Atlantis was in the middle of the Atlantic, and all that is left of the island are its mountains, the peaks of which show through above the waves. Many believe these are now the Azore islands. Evidence also suggests a huge comet or asteroid crashed into the southwest Atlantic Ocean many thousands of years ago, and two holes 23,000 feet deep have been identified on the seabed close to Puerto Rico. Experts believe the impact from such a comet (or comets) would have created massive natural movements, enough to destroy any mid-Atlantic islands.

▶ THE BERMUDA TRIANGLE ◀

The Bermuda Triangle, or Devil's Triangle, is an area of ocean found off the southeastern tip of the United States. This watery region is lastingly connected with mysterious vessel disappearances, and countless boats and planes seem to have been inexplicably lost there. The triangle extends from Bermuda to Miami and then to Puerto Rico, and is said to contain a supernatural secret. Some high-profile disappearances have occurred there, and the notion of its existence has been turned into a modern myth in the media. Even the term "Bermuda Triangle" was coined in a fictional publication. But does this stretch of ocean really house some unknown power that pulls sea- and airmen to their doom, or is this mystery based mainly on imagination?

The most famous loss in the triangle is known as the mystery of Flight 19, and happened on December 5, 1945. A squadron of five US Navy Avenger torpedo bombers set off from their base in Fort Lauderdale, Florida, to conduct a practice mission over the island of Bimini. The flight contained 14 men, all of them students, apart from the commander, Lt. Charles Taylor. Radio operators received a signal from Taylor about an hour and a half after the mission began. He said that his compasses were not working but he believed he was over the Florida Keys. The operators advised him to fly north, which would bring him back to the mainland. It turned out that he was actually over the Bahamas, and his attempts to head north and northeast only took him further away from solid ground. A terrible storm that day hampered communications, and it seems that Taylor rejected a suggestion to pass control of the squadron to one of the other pilots.

Radio contact was entirely lost and search craft were dispatched to try and find the flight to guide it back in. Of the three planes used to rescue Flight 19, one lost communications itself because of an iced over aerial, one was just unsuccessful, and the third seemed to explode shortly after takeoff. Flight 19 itself has never been found, but investigators assumed that the crew ditched into the raging sea when fuel ran out, with the heavy plane rapidly sinking to the ocean floor. The US Navy determined that Taylor's confusion caused the disaster, but his family appealed

32

and the verdict was overturned. A new verdict of "causes or reasons unknown" was given. Flight 19 is not the only high-profile official loss in the area. The USS Cyclops and Marine Sulphur Queen also disappeared without a trace.

The story of Flight 19 was included in the Steven Spielberg movie *Close Encounters of the Third Kind*, which solidified the flight's legend. Some theories postulate that visiting UFO craft (now operating from an underwater base in the Bermuda area) have caused the disappearances. Other far-fetched ideas about technologies from Atlantis or evil marine creatures have also been considered. Some people even suggest that the triangle is the site of a gateway into another dimension. Strange oceanographic features such as huge clouds of methane gas escaping from the seabed have also been blamed for the disappearances.

In reality, the triangle does have one natural quality that may contribute to the losses. Unlike everywhere else in the world—apart from the Dragon's Triangle near Japan—compasses in the triangle point to true north rather than magnetic north. This fact may contribute to the triangle's legend, but the US Coast Guard officially believes that the losses

are caused by a mixture of environmental and man-made mistakes. This region is used by a large amount of ocean and air traffic,

TOP 10 NATURAL EXPLANATIONS FOR DISAPPEARANCES

1. Compass variation: Scientists know compasses point to true north rather than magnetic north.

2. War: Disappearances could be caused by enemy submarines rather than, say, aliens.

3. Pirates: They've been known to sink ships.

4. The Gulf Stream: Its current could carry away a ship or small plane.

5. Human error: Bad judgment or accidents can cause tragedies.

6. Hurricanes: They're pretty destructive. Enough said.

7. Tornadoes: They can be as powerful as hurricanes.

8. Methane gas: Scientists believe gas eruptions can sink ships.

9. Rogue waves: They can destabilize boats and even oil rigs.

10. Trenches: Deep trenches around the Triangle make shipwrecks harder to find.

much of which is navigated by inexperienced pleasure-seekers. A strong Gulf Stream and unpredictable weather conditions not only cause vessels to run into trouble, but also remove many traces of them once they have been wrecked.

Also, the Coast Guard does not view the area as having a particularly high incidence of accidents. One researcher examined many historic losses in the triangle. He concluded that rumors and elaboration have clouded the real, natural causes behind the events. Similarly, the international insurers Lloyd's of London have records that demonstrate that this region near Bermuda is no more treacherous than any other waterway. However, the myth of the Bermuda Triangle is so strong it will live on as long as the media uses it as a site of mysterious happenings.

▶ THE BIBLE CODE ◀

The idea of Bible Codes began in the twelfth century when Jewish students discovered interesting and relevant words hidden in the Hebrew version of the Torah, the first five books of the Bible. Devout Jews believe that details of everything that will ever happen on Earth are recorded here, and the great rabbis have always stressed that, as these writings were dictated by Moses straight from God, no alterations should be made to the text.

The modern era of Bible Codes was begun by Michael Ber Weissmandl, a Slovakian rabbi who narrowly escaped the Nazi death chambers. His interest in ancient books about Bible Codes led him to develop his own theories. Although World War II contributed to ruining Weissmandl's old life, it did promote the idea of code-breakers, with the famous stories of the German Enigma program. It also marked the beginning of microcomputers, and many Torah scholars, fascinated by Weissmandl's ideas, were able to harness complex technology to further the research into Bible Codes.

In 1994 a group of intellectuals, Doron Witztum, Eliyahu Rips, and Yoav Rosenberg, published a study in the journal *Statistical Science* of an experiment they had conducted using methods Weissmandl had developed. They claimed to have found references to 34 great rabbi sages, together with their respective birth and death dates, hidden in the book of Genesis. This study ignited scientific and popular interest in Bible Codes, which is still active today, and has led to many more books being produced, although not all of these have had such groundings in scientific procedures.

So how are the messages in the Bible decoded? In its simplest form, the research uses a system called Equidistant Letter Sequencing. This works by placing all the letters in the text next to each other, with no spaces or punctuation. Then, by performing uniform jumps along the letter chain, other words are discernible. For example:

GENERALIZATION

In the word above, by skipping to every third letter from the starting point, we get the word "NAZI." The method can be used forward or backward, with any number of letter-jumping

G H T E [R] S T H [O] U H A [S] T N O [W] D O N [E] F O O [L] I S H [L] Y I N S

Figure 1. "Roswell" hidden in KJV Genesis 31:28.

"Roswell" hidden in KJV Genesis 31:28.

or spacing. There are even more complicated ways of decoding, called arrays or matrices where a two-dimensional presentation—like a word-search puzzle—that contains hidden words in different directions.

Weissmandl initially discovered that by taking the first "T" in the first verse of the book of Genesis, and then skipping 50 letters three times you end up with the word TVRH, the Hebrew spelling of Torah. This finding applies with the same 50 letter skips in the first verses in the book of Exodus and Numbers. More recent research has shown references to Hitler, *Mein Kampf,* and other historical events. However, sensationalist authors have rather corrupted the system to produce fanciful assertions, and the Bible Code has become a phenomenon rather akin to the prophecies of Nostradamus. Subsequently some researchers have tried to use it as a method of foretelling the future.

Many code enthusiasts believe it is not supposed to be seen as a way of deducing our fate, but should be seen as proof that the Torah was actually written by God, who had knowledge of all that would come to pass. They say that searching the text for references to future events that might occur is not valid, because if they fail to happen, then they would just be random word formations. Many people believe the valid details that do seem to appear in the Bible Code are merely random words that just happen to correspond to real events.

Certainly, there is a huge body of skeptical statistical and computer experts in the scientific world. Two such experts, mathematicians Dror Bar-Natan and Brendan McKay, were the first to refute the findings of Witztum, Rips, and Rosenberg. McKay and Bar-Natan found similar results when looking for the details of famous rabbis within the text of Tolstoy's *War and Peace.*

The Bible Code–breakers say they are pursuing this subject to prove God actually did write the Bible, although one is tempted to think that an overly elaborate code system would have little effect on the faith of either a believer or an atheist.

▶ THE BIG BANG ◀

The greatest, most fundamental mystery in the history of the world is the question of how "it" all began? We now know a lot about the different stages of Earth's development, but we still have no definite answers for how our world came to be or even how the universe was formed. Religion provides us with one theory—the idea that God created the planets by hand, but that does not tally with the few pieces of scientific evidence that we do have. And, although we are still largely ignorant, science has begun to reveal some of the secrets of the cosmos. We do not know much, but we do know it all started with a bang. The Big Bang.

About 15 billion years ago there was an enormous explosion. Incredible, trillion-degree heat, matter, and antimatter were all created in a dense, expanding cloud. In less than 1/1,000th of a second, the universe had doubled in size over 100 times. The explosion produced more matter than antimatter, and basic particles began to form. The universe remained a thick, plasmatic substance, made up mainly of radiation at an extreme, but cooling, heat. After a second, the universe had a temperature of almost 18 billion degrees Fahrenheit. The process continued, with simple particles gradually slowing in speed, allowing for more complex reactions to take place.

About three minutes after the initial explosion, the temperature was down to a billion degrees. Nucleosynthesis was beginning to take place, and deuterium, an isotope also known as heavy hydrogen, was being created. Deuterium then formed into tritium, which

DID YOU KNOW...WE MAY HAVE FIGURED IT OUT?

Scientists at CERN, the European Organization for Nuclear Research, have been hard at work trying to, essentially, re-create the Big Bang, using a massive particle accelerator called the Large Hadron Collider. They believe this experiment will uncover what's known as the "God particle," or Higgs boson, which would explain how elementary particles get their mass, and bring us closer to understanding the origins of the universe. As of December 2011, scientists were incredibly close to confirming the particle's existence, and we could be closer to learning where we came from after all.

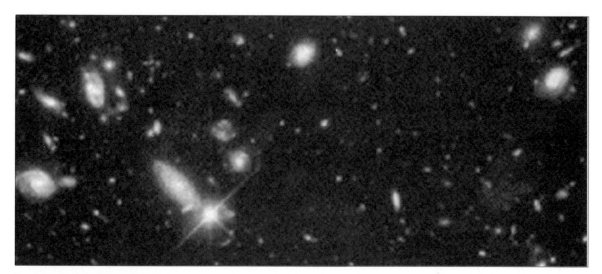

The Big Bang: older than radio.

then became a helium nucleus. With slightly more cooling, hydrogen atoms were created. Over the next 300,000 years, helium atoms formed, and the universe dropped to a temperature of ten thousand degrees Fahrenheit as it expanded. Radiation gradually became less dense and light and matter were able to separate. Eventually, after 15 billion years, the universe became what we know today.

Although the Big Bang theory is based on the guesswork of many eminent cosmologists and astronomers, it has a scientific basis. Recent discoveries have also helped to provide proof. NASA's COBE satellite has detected cosmic microwaves produced at the distant edges of the universe. The fact that these microwaves follow a similarly rigid structure suggests that the universe developed in a verifiable pattern. Slight temperature differences at three far-off points have also helped to prove scientists' earlier theories about what happened as the cosmos cooled. The different stages in development between areas of different heat give a good indication of what happened following the Big Bang.

In June 1995, scientists working on NASA's Astro-2 observatory were able to detect deuterium in the distant corners of the cosmos.

This suggests that such elements really did exist soon after the Big Bang. Similarly, the Hubble telescope has allowed astronomers to look deep into the universe and discover what substances are predominant in older features. These new discoveries often lead to new questions, and the reworking of old theories. What we can be certain of is that the universe continues to expand, so the Big Bang phenomenon is still in progress. The fact that these procedures are still in effect at the far reaches of the universe provides hope that, as our observational techniques improve, we will definitely be able to learn how the universe initially expanded.

As intelligent life forms, we may feel confident enough to scientifically determine the conditions at the dawn of time and space. However, no scientist would dare to suggest exactly what existed before the Big Bang. Religious philosophers have stated that everything has a cause, and have used our ignorance of the subject as proof of God. Others state that not all happenings necessarily have a catalyst, and as we are entering a completely new realm of the unknown, the normal rules of the universe may not apply.

In either case, that is a subject for philosophy, rather than physics or chemistry. What science can say is that everything around us is made up of particles that burst from an original source even smaller than an atom, 15 billion years ago. Everything else remains a mystery.

► BIGFOOT ◄

There are stories of a mystical, apelike creature roaming in the wilds of North America, and hiding in the shadows. It should be hard to stay concealed at over seven feet tall with an immense, muscled body, but many that see him say he disappears into the background. Like a man, he walks upright, but the short black hair covering his body indicates he is no homo sapiens. No bodies, bones, or remains have ever been found despite more than two centuries of searching. The only evidence we have of this mythical beast is its huge tracks. That's why the creature is called "Bigfoot."

Bigfoot never was a fan of pants.

Like many legendary Native American monsters, Bigfoot is a central part of indigenous traditional tales. Native Americans called him "Sasquatch," the "hairy giant of the woods." But it was his early introduction to European settlers that sparked real interest. In 1811, David Thompson, a British trader, was in the Rocky Mountains when he spotted a set of massive 14-by-8-inch footprints. Over many years, tales of Sasquatch spread and on July 4, 1884, the *Daily Colonist* newspaper in British Columbia announced that a train crew had caught a strange beast. In reality, the stocky, black-haired primate that they trapped was probably just a chimpanzee.

The American and Canadian mountains gradually grew awash with stories of Sasquatch appearances, and there were even reports of gangs of strange creatures attacking people in the forests. But the Sasquatch phenomenon was never limited to the idea of a single mutant creature and people have always considered that there might be a breeding colony. Early on, the mystical beasts were primarily of interest to lumberjacks, miners, and those who lived or worked in areas where they had been sighted.

That changed in 1958 when Jerry Crew, a bulldozer operator working in Humboldt County, California, made casts of bizarre footprints he had found. A local newspaper photographed Crew, and his picture was syndicated nationwide. The sight of a man holding a plaster cast of the mysterious tracks started the modern Bigfoot legend. But if Crew's discovery helped to launch the myth, it was an episode nine years later that sealed Bigfoot's place in American consciousness.

In October 1967, Roger Patterson and Bob Gimlin were riding on horseback through Bluff Creek, California, when, according to their account, a Bigfoot suddenly appeared in their path. They were in the area specifically looking for Bigfoot, so it wasn't completely unexpected, but Patterson's horse was certainly surprised, and threw Patterson off. Gimlin, however, kept a rifle trained on the beast, while Patterson regained his footing and ran toward the creature, filming all the time with a movie camera they had brought with them. The result is perhaps the most compelling piece of evidence yet. The footage shows a large hairy biped slowly strolling into the undergrowth.

Although the evidence is startling, many have questioned its authenticity. Some experts believe, if the film is played at a slightly faster speed, it could easily be a human in a costume. However, aspects of the footage are pretty amazing. For example, biotechnology scientists have said that for a creature like Bigfoot to walk upright it would

DID YOU KNOW...YOU CAN CATCH YOUR OWN BIGFOOT?

Try these tips from the experts:

* Find a quiet, low-traffic area.
* Use fresh meat or veggies and fruit as bait. There is evidence that spoiled food and fish gross him out.
* Be consistent—bait him every morning.
* Entice him with other stuff, such as wind chimes or a salt block.
* Hang back until Bigfoot is relaxed before you try to take his picture.
* Take good notes! You never know when you'll need to convince someone of a Bigfoot sighting.

need an extended heel, which the creature on the film actually has.

Experts in the industry initially expected the film to be merely special effects, but they have been unable to find any telltale signs that it is a hoax. Similarly, a group of Russian scientists who attempted to determine the correct speed of the film concluded that the creature really did have a long, lumbering gait. However, Gimlin himself has entertained the possibility that he might have been an unwitting participant in a hoax orchestrated by his friend. We'll never know for sure, since Patterson died of cancer in 1972.

More recent sightings of the ape-man have taken on a new and bizarre twist. People have reported seeing UFOs in the regions of Bigfoot appearances. Also, the creatures are now said to carry glowing orbs, and have bright red eyes. This may seem a strange twist, but Sasquatches were always reported as having a quality beyond the physical, and it has been suggested that when they die, Bigfoot bodies vanish into the ether. This is a shame, because to really accept Bigfoot's presence, the world needs to see some hard, physical evidence.

The ape-man thinks it's pretty rude when random tourists interrupt his nature walk.

► CROP CIRCLES ◄

We regard the phenomenon of crop circles as being a relatively recent mystery, but strange patterns have actually appeared in fields for over 300 years. Sometimes they occur in sand, ice, or even snow. Five thousand of these odd geometric shapes have manifested themselves in over 40 countries across the globe. However, we are still no closer to understanding their significance. Some are undoubtedly hoaxes, but what do the others mean? Are they messages from space, Mother Earth, or perhaps another dimension?

Those who live in the countryside, particularly those who live along ley lines and channels of natural energy, have come

DID YOU KNOW...IT MAY NOT BE THE ALIENS AFTER ALL?

Australian wildlife has recently developed some unusual habits. Wallabies have been eating the poppies that grow on opium plants, which are abundant in Australia—the country produces about half of the world's legally grown opium—and the opium consumption has been making the critters act... well...strange. The creatures tend to go walking in the opium fields after eating the plants, creating crop circles similar to the ones that have baffled scientists for hundreds of years. Apparently sheep do this too, though it's not clear whether they enjoy the opium as much.

to regard the circles as part of rural life. A few witnesses have actually seen them made. They say that an invisible line snakes its way at high speed through a field, pushing the stalks of crops aside. It begins to spin around when it reaches a certain point, pushing the crop down radially, as the hands on a clock would. When it has turned a full 360 degrees the force just vanishes, leaving the crop perfectly matted on the field floor. No stalks spring up, and no stalks are crushed. They are all carefully and permanently bowed.

Who or what actually determines that the patterns should be made is still up for debate. Tales of UFOs and odd lights above fields the night before new formations appear are common. There are also a substantial number of hoax circles, but these are often easily discernible, since they have trampled, crushed crops rather than gently bent stalks.

Many people are convinced that freak weather conditions, such as mini, localized whirlwinds, cause the patterns. Investigators are also studying the scientific qualities of crop circles, and they hope a rational, serious approach will reveal the truth.

Perhaps the most popular explanation for the appearance of crop circles is connected with earth forces. The great majority of good, reputable patterns in England appear in Wiltshire, around historic areas of high natural energy. They also often occur close to ancient forts, burial mounds, standing stones, and fertility symbols, suggesting an affiliation with Britain's traditional heritage. In fact, many people are convinced the ancient forces of Mother Earth have a hand in the creation of crop circles.

Crop circles also appear to have a quirky effect on electronic equipment. Tape recorders have been known to speed up once they're inside a circle and then slow down outside. State-of-the-art video equipment malfunctions without good cause, and even ordinary cameras can produce severely distorted images. Circles also have a rather strange effect on farm machinery. Not only are good crops flattened during a circle's production, but many farmers have seen their harvesting equipment stop working near the circles.

The circles have striking effects on humans, too. Some experts suggest that stepping inside certain patterns can cause extreme emotional change. Some people feel an improved sense of physical well-being and vitality in certain circles, while others experience feelings of nausea, fatigue, light-headedness, and even migraines. People with long-standing medical conditions are said to have experienced significant improvement or have even been cured just by sitting inside crop circles. Circles have an equally impressive effect on animals. Horses and cats in particular become agitated near patterns, and often refuse to enter them. Flocks of

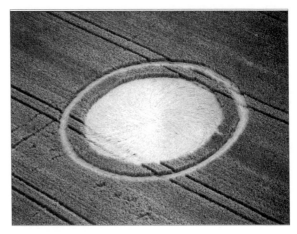

A relatively uncomplicated crop circle set-up.

birds have been seen flying straight toward a crop formation, only to drastically steer around them at the last minute. Some dogs feel compelled to bound right into the center of some circles, only to drop down asleep when they reach them.

Hoax crop circles can be frustrating because, of all unexplained phenomena, circles are one of the most deserving of further study. Crop circles are their own record of some unknown power. Whatever causes these formations undoubtedly leaves a trace of its inexplicable force. Country people have grown to live with whatever has gone on in their fields for centuries, but it is still something they do not quite understand.

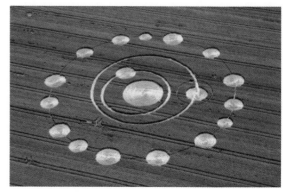

But what does it *mean*?

► CRYSTALS ◄

The New Age movement places great emphasis on one particular type of power instrument: crystals. New Age believers regard these attractive chemical solidifications as being the wonder substance of New Age belief. Crystals have also permeated the world of popular culture. The celebrity world is awash with high profile, spiritually aware people who attest to the positive power of crystals. They believe these substances direct and control energy flows in the body and promote physical and emotional well-being. But do crystals really provide magical support for people or is this effect merely an unsubstantiated craze?

A crystal is a solid, rock-like substance created by chemicals solidifying in a solution. Its chemical construction is particularly special because it is formed by regularly repeating patterns of atoms and molecules, and the crystal particle is pulled together by flat external forces. Like snowflakes, crystals are a naturally occurring phenomenon and each one is unique, occurring in any number of shapes. They are highly aesthetic and prized for use in clothing and jewelry.

Throughout history, people have regarded crystals as having magic properties and holding bizarre paranormal powers. Ancient people thought crystals contained the power of Mother Earth as they originated in its crust, and also the energy of the sun because they reflect light in bizarre ways. Crystals were also supposed to show the future and give people superhuman powers. Psychics' use of crystal balls was a deliberate choice.

Modern New Age enthusiasts believe the power of crystals lies in their ability to regulate, calm, and heal the body. They believe crystals channel good energy, ward off bad energy, and vibrate at frequencies that complement natural body functions. Lifestyle gurus declare that crystals promote self-expression, meditation, and creativity, and that a full complement of different crystals is needed to engage with all a person's needs.

Different crystals are said to affect the body in different ways. Amethysts are believed to help headaches, balance blood sugar levels, increase psychic abilities, reduce anger, impatience, nightmares, and help with eye and hair problems. Emeralds apparently increase the efficiency of a body's respiration, heart, and blood systems, lift depression and insomnia, and evoke peace, harmony, patience, and love. Finally, diamonds increase clarity, confidence, and trust, clarify attitudes and thoughts, and develop prosperity, generosity, and love. What better reason could there be for buying crystals for a loved one?

In recent years it has been fashionable to employ crystals in jewelry, not only for aesthetic qualities, but also to have beneficial power sources near the body. A chiropractor called Charles Brown developed the Bioelectric Shield—a piece of jewelry with

Crystals love to just hang out together. They find each other's company to be very soothing.

SPOTLIGHT ON...
THE CRYSTAL SKULL

The Mitchell-Hedges crystal skull is probably the most famous of the few that have been found. It's life-sized and made of quartz crystal. Explorer F. A. Mitchell-Hedges, the real-life inspiration for Indiana Jones, claimed to have found the skull, supposedly in a Mayan ruin. Its owners say it was brought to earth by aliens, has unique psychic properties, and can show the future. So far, scientists haven't been able to determine where it came from or how it was made. Maybe time—or another explorer like Indiana Jones—will tell.

its crystals arranged in such a way that they protect people from all the many harmful electromagnetic forces in the modern world: mobile phones, computer screens, and power lines. These "shields" are said to be medically proven, and even Cherie Blair, the wife of former British Prime Minister Tony Blair, wears them. The different constructions of these shields are said to provide protection for different things.

Unfortunately, these assertions have no scientific basis. They are actually based on nothing more than blind faith. Skeptics believe any effect they do have on human beings is the result of selective or wishful thinking, more self-deception and placebo effect. But crystals do have many vital roles in our modern world. They are important components in electronic, optical, and communication industries, and feature in many types of high-tech equipment. This is due to one special function that some crystals really do have: Producing an electrical change when they are compressed. This quality was first discovered in 1880 by Pierre and Jacques Curie and was termed the piezoelectric effect. Now crystals are used for highly scientific purposes.

However, the piezoelectric effect has no effect on the human body, and there is no evidence that crystals provide any protection from illness, calamity, or misfortune. That does not detract from their beauty, but as far as science is concerned the magical power of crystals is completely unfounded.

► THE DEAD SEA SCROLLS ◄

The northern shore of the Dead Sea is a particularly dry, arid place. It is 13 miles from Jerusalem, and even though the area is often shrouded in haze, the humidity levels are extremely low: It is the perfect place to preserve ancient artifacts. In the spring of 1947, two young Bedouin shepherds were looking for a lost goat among the cliffs in the area known as Qumran. As they hunted from cave to cave, they came upon a store of jars containing many papyrus and parchment manuscripts. These scrolls only came to prominence later that year when members of the Bedouin community sold seven of the texts to a local antiquities dealer. As the academic world heard about the discovery, intense excitement burst through the global community of historians. They were right to be excited: This would turn out to be the most important discovery of ancient scrolls in the twentieth century.

In 1949 the exact location of the initial find was discovered, and the cave was thoroughly surveyed. Archaeologists discovered more fragments of scrolls, along with pieces of cloth, pottery, and wood. Over the next seven years they found ancient texts in ten more caves in the Qumran area, and they discovered the remains of around 850 different scrolls in total. The caves were named in the order that they were searched, and cave four, uncovered in 1952, produced the single biggest haul of artifacts with 15,000 fragments of 500 different manuscripts. A complex of ancient structures close to the caves, referred to as the Qumran ruin, was also excavated.

A page from the Dead Sea Scrolls.

He gets to smoke while handling precious, brittle documents? Who's managing this guy?

Scientists discovered that the scrolls and the ruin both dated from between the third century BCE and 68 CE, placing them around the time of Christ. It seems the texts formed the library of a Jewish sect, possibly the Essenes. The Essenes—a strict, Torah-observing society—disliked the established priesthood, and may have actually been wiped out by the Jerusalem-based church. It is thought that the ruins at Qumran formed part of their society, and Essenes hid the scrolls from the advancing Roman army around 70 CE.

What the scrolls contain is even more fascinating than their history. The scrolls have been deciphered and reconstructed by expert modern scholars, and they tend to fall into two groups: texts concerned with religion and texts revealing details of daily life and history. They include copies of many biblical writings, and all but one book of the Old Testament. More interestingly, the scrolls contain previously unseen psalms authored by King David and Joshua, and also some prophecies attributed to Ezekiel, Jeremiah, and Daniel that do not appear in the Bible.

The scrolls contain previously unknown stories about Enoch, Abraham, and Noah. Similarly the lost words of Amram, Joseph, Judah, Levi, and Naphtali are revealed in the texts.

Surprisingly, given their date and proximity to New Testament events, the scrolls do not mention the life of Jesus Christ. The scrolls are mainly written in Hebrew, but also feature passages in Aramaic and Greek. Some scrolls explain laws and codes of battle, while others recount poems and the philosophies of wise men. The most enigmatic information contained in the scrolls lists 64 places around Israel where ancient treasures are buried. It is suggested that not only are gold and silver hidden there, but that many of the holy objects from the temple of Jerusalem were also deposited in distant, unknown places for safekeeping.

Although the scrolls were all discovered within eight years, the collection was scattered among universities, museums, and scholarly institutions across the world. In 1954, some of the scrolls were even advertised for sale in the *Wall Street Journal*. Many of the scrolls were in terrible condition, so it became difficult to assemble a complete idea of what the texts revealed. During the 1960s and 1970s much of the work that was done remained unpublished, so public interest in the scrolls waned. In the last decade however, there has been a renewed commitment to provide complete collections of photographs, translations, and explanations to the world. This seems vitally important. Not only do the scrolls represent an amazing historical discovery, they also chronicle a time essential to our understanding of the biblical world.

FUN FACTS:

As with many mysterious discoveries, the Dead Sea Scrolls have been used to support some very strange theories. Some examples of these are:

* ☀ Jesus, John the Baptist, and the apostle James were enemies of St. Paul
* ☀ John the Baptist was in a fight with Jesus.
* ☀ Jesus took heavy meds to fake his death on the cross.
* ☀ The entire concept of Christianity was developed under the influence of mushroom-induced hallucinations.

As it happens, the scrolls don't mention Jesus at all, but proponents remain convinced.

► DEMONIC POSSESSION ◄

Theologians believe the idea of possession began with the Zoroastrian religion in Persia, but the continual references to the phenomenon in the teachings of Jesus sealed the concept as a major spiritual occurrence. A survey conducted in 2002 revealed that 54 percent of Americans believed in the genuine power of unwelcome spiritual forces to control a person. Many people believe that the idea of of possession just refers to our naturally occuring desires, and temptations. But surely otherworldly forces cannot really inhabit the human mind? Right?

Something bizarre does seem to happen to people who become fixated with the occult. Possession is believed to happen over a gradual period of time. As time passes, so the possessed person gradually loses control over his actions. To begin with, the invading spirit can be pleasant and helpful, but as soon as the host body tells it to leave, legend has it that the spirit becomes hateful and spiteful.

The possession gradually becomes more total. It results in the possessed person becoming isolated and aggressive. The person's behavior increases in its unpredictability, and he or she suffers from terrible nightmares, sleeplessness, and headaches. Finally, the fear that the spirit's power is uncontrollable can drive the possessed person to attempt suicide, or to be locked in a mental hospital.

If caught in time, the possessed person can be exorcised by a priest, but this process is

DID YOU KNOW...THE CATHOLIC CHURCH STILL PERFORMS EXORCISMS?

Movies like *The Exorcist* can convince us that the devil only inhabits Hollywood. But Catholic priests say that, though rare, exorcism is alive and well in the twenty-first century. In fact, some say that the church is actually looking for more exorcists—several dioceses are holding seminars and offering training in the practice. The church updated its guidelines in 1999 to emphasize ruling out psychiatric illness first. But if the person in question starts speaking in strange languages, demonstrates unusual strength, and suddenly hates holy water—it might be time to call a priest.

A medieval engraving of holy men casting out demons…and of (surprisingly adorable) demonic pigs taking a bath.

so strenuous that it has also been known to kill the victim.

In 2002, an American woman named Andrea Yates claimed demonic possession had caused her to kill her five children. Yates drowned the children, ranging in age from six months to seven years, in June 2001 and pleaded not guilty by reason of insanity.

Many experts believe possession is nothing more than an outlet for severe mental difficulties. Just as biblical possession may represent impure desires, so real-life possession may represent psychosis. Whatever the case, possession is a dangerous state of mind that needs immediate professional help—whether priestly or medical—to restore the mental balance of its unfortunate victim.

► DOWSING ◄

The image of a man with a forked stick searching for water is very well known. Initially he finds nothing, but as he approaches a tree, some strong power starts pulling the end of the stick downward. The man looks triumphant, his talent and techniques vindicated. He has found a well. The process the man used is called dowsing, and it can be used to find water, oil, gold, and even golf balls. It is known as one of the oldest of psychic powers, and connects man directly with the earth—but does dowsing really work?

Over the centuries, dowsers have repeatedly appeared in human cultures and traditions. It is said that cave drawings in Spain and Iraq show dowsers working in prehistoric times, and woodcuts from ancient China and Britain support the long heritage of dowsing. During the Middle Ages, people vilified dowsers as witches or devil worshippers. Martin Luther even claimed that dowsing was "the work of the devil." However, history also shows that many official groups have placed their trust in dowsers. German dowsers were apparently invited to assist British miners during the reign of Queen Elizabeth I, and it is claimed that modern military organizations actively employ them. General Patton was said to have used dowsers to find water to replace the wells destroyed by German forces during World War II. Similarly, the US Marine Corps apparently used dowsers to find mines hidden during the Vietnam War, and the British Army followed suit in the Falklands Islands.

Most dowsers employ a very simple method to find what they're looking for. First, they

DID YOU KNOW...YOU CAN ALSO DOWSE FOR GHOSTS?

Despite the lack of any scientific support, some people are trying to find ghosts with dowsing rods, too! Websites advertising dowsing rods proclaim that the rods can find ghosts, spirits, and even unmarked graves. They say that the dowsing rods detect the physical manifestations of the energy that ghosts give off. The sites recommend different approaches and sell different types of rods for a variety of ghost hunting situations. But they all agree on one thing: Practice makes perfect.

walk around a specified area while holding their dowsing tools. These can be forked branches that point down when the dowser is standing above the desired resource, or, more commonly, two L-shaped rods made of copper, wood, or wire—one held in each hand. The rods sit in the palms of the dowser with the longest side of the "L" pointing forward. When the dowser approaches the hunted resource, the rods swivel in the palm to touch each other, forming a cross. Another method of dowsing involves using a piece of string with a crystal on the end. The pendulum gently swings and the dowser is subtly guided to what he or she is looking for. In a most impressive display, some dowsers are not even physically in the area they're searching in, and they simply use their dowsing technique over a map to locate an object.

There are a number of theories as to why the rods move. Some believe it is caused by electromagnetic power or other earth forces, but most proponents feel that dowsing is not controlled by physical or chemical influences, but more by the inherent ability of the dowser. It is suggested that, over time and with practice, dowsers can improve their talents and success rate. There have been some striking results from experienced dowsers. In a

When this kid goes dowsing, he puts his game face on.

1995 report by Hans-Dieter Betz, a physicist at the University of Munich, it was claimed that some dowsers achieved a 96 percent success rate in 691 drilling attempts to find water in Sri Lanka. The German government has since sponsored one hundred dowsers to find water in arid areas of southern India.

The conventional scientific view is, however, that dowsing achieves no better results than pure guesswork. Indeed, there are a handful of high-profile competitions involving big money prizes for dowsers. One such challenge promises a million dollars for an 80 percent success rate in finding water flowing through underground pipes during controlled conditions. The money has never been won.

Some dowsers do use their skills to earn a healthy living—a select few act as advisors to mining and drilling companies searching for minerals. However, the fact is that scientists are always skeptical about phenomena that they cannot explain. But the great thing about dowsing, unlike other psychic powers, is that it is an activity anyone can at least try. Who knows, if you practice hard enough, there may be a million dollar check just waiting to be cashed!

► DRACULA ◄

Eastern Europe in the Middle Ages was a turbulent place. The great nation of Hungary was its first line of defense against Ottoman forces, and the individual states that happened to be located in the no man's land between the two suffered terrible unrest. It was enough to inspire Bram Stoker to write his most famous novel, although people now wonder which figure during this unstable period influenced Stoker the most. Only one name truly stands out—the real, terrible man known as Dracula.

Wallachia, now part of Romania, was a Hungarian province ruled by Prince Mircea the Elder until 1418. In around 1390, Mircea had an illegitimate son named Vlad who was given away to be brought up in the court of Hungary's King Sigismund. When Mircea died, Vlad was not given control of Wallachia, but he was made a Knight of the Order of the Dragon, a group set up to defend the Christian world from Turkish rule. Vlad was soon given the name Dracul, meaning "dragon," and made governor of Transylvania.

Dracul had three sons. The first, named after his father Mircea, was born in 1443, with the next two named Vlad and Radu. Dracul gathered an army and took back his family's traditional seat of power in Wallachia, although only with the help of their old enemy, Turkey.

Dracula is notorious for his violations of personal space. Stop being such a close-talker, Dracula!

As a sign of his loyalty, Dracul sent Vlad and Radu to live in Adrianople, the seat of the Ottoman Empire. In 1447 Dracul and Mircea were killed, and a Hungarian government again ruled Wallachia. This situation made the Turkish rulers uncomfortable, so in 1448 they decided to arm the seventeen-year-old Vlad, who was known as the "Son of Dragon," or Dracula.

Over the next several years the fighting continued, but by 1456 Dracula had reclaimed his throne in Wallachia. He built a capital city at Tirgoviste and was pronounced Prince Vlad III. From the beginning, he realized that to survive he would have to be utterly ruthless. Shortly after he was crowned prince, he invited destitute souls from the streets of his kingdom to a great feast at his castle. After the meal, he asked the assembled poor, frail, and aged if they would "like to be without cares, lacking nothing in the world?" When they all cried yes, he promptly boarded up the castle and set it on fire. He said there was little place in his society for people who would be a burden, and anybody who did not contribute to the community should receive little sympathy.

Killing the infirm was a message to the general public, but Dracula took similar action with Wallachia's dignitaries. He had the older ones impaled, and sent the others to build a castle at Poenari, a mountainous area fifty

miles away. In their place, Dracula organized his own set of nobles to confirm his power. His cruelty knew no bounds, and he particularly enjoyed watching people die from being hoisted onto sharpened poles. His people called him Vlad Tepes, meaning "Vlad

CHRONOLOGY: EVOLUTION OF FICTIONAL VAMPS

Bram Stoker's Dracula created the most legendary vampire ever. But the character of Dracula—although always recognizable—has undergone a lot of changes since then. Included below is a timeline of the most iconic vampires

- ✳ 1922: *Nosferatu*, an iconic Dracula film adaptation with a vampire that looks like a bat.
- ✳ 1931: Bella Lugosi as Dracula, a prototype for all future fictional vampires.
- ✳ 1972–present: *Sesame Street*'s Count, modeled after Lugosi's Dracula.
- ✳ 1973–2004: The comic superhero Blade, a vampire hunter who was also half vampire.
- ✳ 1976–2003: Lestat, the vain antihero of Anne Rice's *The Vampire Chronicles*.
- ✳ 2005–present: Edward Cullen, moody star of the *Twilight* saga.
- ✳ 2009–present: *The Vampire Diaries*: The most brooding and attractive vamps on TV.

the Impaler," and the Turkish knew him as Kaziglu Bey or the "Impaler Prince." He murdered cheating wives, fraudulent merchants, and anybody who committed any crime. He also enjoyed skinning and boiling people alive. He killed children and the elderly, and put their bodies on public display to warn would-be criminals. It is said that 20,000 dead bodies hung from the walls of Tirgoviste, and by the end of his reign he had killed around 50,000 people.

In 1462, when the Turks—led by Dracula's younger brother, Radu—attacked Wallachia, Dracula went into exile in Hungary. In 1476, with Radu dead of syphilis and another prince on Wallachia's throne, Dracula attempted to regain his rightful home. He succeeded, but was killed in December 1476 during another Turkish attack. The Ottoman sultan impaled Dracula's head and had it displayed in Constantinople as evidence of his death. His body was said to have been buried in an island monastery called Snagov, although investigative digs in 1931 were unable to produce the coffin. It's yet another mystery in Dracula's terrifying story.

Some proof of his reign does remain, however. His fortress in the hills of Poenari stands today as a popular tourist destination, and there are also ruins of his palace at Tirgoviste. More important than any physical heritage is his memory in the minds of the Romanian people.

Dracula's behavior was so horrific that we probably shouldn't be surprised that it was the inspiration for the most famous vampire story of all time: Bram Stoker's novel *Dracula*, published in 1897. Vampire folklore had already been around for centuries—several ancient cultures told of demons that drank blood or ate human flesh. But vampire hysteria exploded in rural Eastern European villages in the eighteenth century, when people began reporting sightings of creatures that were "undead." This fear, which began as a vague phenomenon, developed to the point where people became convinced that these undead creatures could exist for eternity by drinking the blood of the living.

Bram Stoker's novel was influenced by vampire legends, but it popularized the modern stereotype of a vampire as pale, tall, and thin. Stroker's Count Dracula is intelligent and aristocratic, but he also has sharp teeth, unusual strength, and is prone to occasional fits of rage. Count Dracula is powerful, but can be affected by holy water, garlic, and sunlight—and can be killed by silver bullets or wooden stakes. At first he seems charming, but his evil intentions are revealed gradually throughout the novel. It will have to be up to the reader to decide which man was more evil—the fictional Count…or the real-life Dracula.

► EASTER ISLAND ◄

Easter Island, or Rapa Nui, is in the South Pacific Ocean, about 2,300 miles from the west coast of Peru. It was formed by a volcanic eruption on the ocean floor, and is separated from the other Polynesian islands by huge expanses of sea. The island occupies 45 square miles, and has three volcanic craters, which are now lakes. The lakes are some of the few fertile areas, for the rest of the island is rather desolate and barren. However, it has not always been like this and there is evidence that the land was once rich in flora and fauna.

The outside world first heard about Easter Island when a Dutch admiral named Jakob Roggeveen stumbled across it on Easter Sunday, 1722. When he landed, he found a native race, the Rapanui, that seemed to be suffering from diminished natural resources. What really amazed him, though, were the huge stone-carved figures, or *moai*, that stood on guard around the island. Modern investigations have revealed there are something like one thousand of these great statues, standing between 12 and 25 feet high, and weighing up to 22 tons. The largest one is 65 feet tall and weighs 99 tons. However, when Roggeveen stepped ashore, many of these figures had already been torn down by the natives.

The origin of the Rapanui is an issue of contention. Another early visitor to the island was Captain James Cook. Cook had a Hawaiian sailor aboard his ship who could understand the Easter Island native tongue. This suggested that the natives spoke Polynesian, and the general consensus is that they were descended from a distant Polynesian tribe. There is also a theory that they actually came from South America,

DID YOU KNOW...THEY HAVE BODIES TOO?

There's more to the moai than giant heads and tiny torsos. The Easter Island Statue Project, which studies artifacts on the island, has uncovered actual bodies attached to several of the heads. Many have been buried underground for hundreds of years. Though most of the statues still don't have legs, they are much bigger—and more proportional—than people think. Many of the statues also wore hats or topknots called *pukao*. The pukao may represent tribal chief headdresses—or thirteenth-century hairstyles.

which is supported by the fact that the bulrushes and sweet potatoes found on the island were said to be imports from that continent. There were also considerable similarities between pre-Inca American cultures and the examples of Easter Island culture, although it is believed that there may have been an early trading industry between Easter Island, South America, and the Polynesian Islands.

The Rapanui probably settled on the island sometime around the middle of the first millennium CE, and began building their statues soon afterward. The early islanders developed a precise technique for creating the stone men out of the walls of the volcanic craters. They used a system of logs and ropes to sit the moai on a funerary platform, called an *ahu*, under which the remains of dead elders were buried. It is believed that the stone figure acted as a talisman, guarding and protecting the clan of the dead islander, although some experts suggest the islanders ended up erecting the statues purely for the joy of making them. Archaeologists have also discovered wooden tablets called "talking boards," which describe ancient religious rites of the old culture.

According to this man's measuring technique, the Easter Island statues are as tall as "me plus a stick... plus a little more."

The Easter Island story is the archetypal island version of paradise lost. When the first Polynesian immigrants landed on the island it was a land of bountiful natural produce. There were great forests, sugar beet crops, exotic fruit, and native meat sources. The people flourished in these conditions. They built fine houses and enjoyed life, but in around 1500 a new cult called *Makemake* or "the cult of the birdman" sprang up. This may have signaled the arrival of a new tribe from across the sea, and soon afterward overpopulation and wasteful island management made the crops fail and depleted the natural resources. The different clans and tribes began warring, even overturning each other's statues, and legend on the island recounts a terrible battle between tribes of "long ears" and a tribe of "short ears."

The stone heads do not have the most active social life. This is their typical New Year's Eve. Get a life, stone heads!

Within a couple of centuries, Easter Island was the barren wasteland discovered by Roggeveen—and after Roggeveen's arrival things only grew worse. The intertribal conflicts continued until 1862, when ships arrived and enslaved one thousand of the island's fit men to work in the Peruvian mining industry. These islanders quickly grew ill on the strange continent, and the few that returned home brought back diseases. Smallpox and leprosy reduced the native population to 111 by 1877. European missionary workers helped the people of Easter Island to survive, but many of the secrets of the island's strange stone faces were lost forever.

► EL DORADO ◄

When the Conquistadors were ravaging and looting the ancient cultures of the Aztecs and Incas, native tribesmen told them about an amazing rumor. They said that there was a race, deep in the jungle, whose king was covered with gold dust and who swam in a golden lake. It was the story of El Dorado, the Golden Man. One of the first Spaniards to set off to find this fantasy land was a man named Jimenez de Quesada. In 1536, Quesada and 500 soldiers hacked into the undergrowth from the northwest of what is now Colombia. After many hard days trudging through intense and dangerous jungle, they came upon two tribes of Chibchas, a people with plentiful riches. The Chibchas had gold, silver, and huge amounts of emeralds, but they did not have the fabled El Dorado. However, they told Quesada of a very interesting lake, located not far away, in the middle of a huge volcanic crater on the Bogota plateau.

The Chibchas revealed that the lake was called Guatavita, and they told of a bizarre annual ceremony of "the Golden Man." Chibcha witnesses said the occasion was used to offer sacrifices and gifts to the people's god. The king was smeared in sticky mud and covered with gold dust. He and four other chiefs then sailed on a raft with their finest jewels and treasures, while the tribe played music at the shoreline. When the king and his party reached the center of the lake they threw the offerings into the water, and the king then bathed himself to remove his golden covering. Quesada travelled to the lake, but could find no clues that hinted at treasure. Other Spaniards heard the rumors about Guatavita, and attempted to dredge the lake in 1545.

As the years passed, each new expedition heard other versions of the El Dorado legend. Each one ploughed into the jungle certain they would find the wealth. None ever did, but they did come across other interesting things. In 1537, one adventurer, Francisco de Orellana, was trying to find the golden city by sailing down the Napo River. Orellana reached the end of the Napo, and realized it was a tributary to another, massive river. As he floated along, a tribe of long-haired, fierce female archers attacked his boat. The women reminded Orellano of the Amazons of Scythia in Greek legend, and he named the river "Amazonas."

In 1584 another native rumor appeared. It suggested that Incas fleeing from the Spanish invaders had created a new city of gold called Manoa. This became inseparable from the El Dorado legend, and in 1595 the British adventurer Sir Walter Raleigh attempted to find Manoa and its gold for Queen Elizabeth I. He failed, and a further fruitless expedition in 1617 helped to seal his execution. Over the years, yet another myth circulated—that of a lost mystical lake called Parima. It was described as being almost identical to Quesada's initial discovery, Lake Guatavita. More expeditions floundered in the jungle, haphazardly slicing their way through the foliage until they ran out of supplies, funds, men, or patience.

Meanwhile, other Spaniards had decided to continue trying to reach the bottom of Lake Guatavita. In the 1580s, Antonio de Sepulveda, a merchant living in Bogota, used 8,000 native men to drain the lake by cutting a huge gash in the side. He did manage to remove a fair deal of water, and found considerable gold, but the earth walls collapsed, killing many workmen. He was forced to abandon the project. Further attempts to drain the lake continued right into the twentieth century, and many historically valuable artifacts were found, but never the great quantities of treasure promised by the legends.

SPOTLIGHT ON...THE EL DORADO MYTH IN POP CULTURE

Like the mythical fountain of youth, El Dorado has become a fixture in pop culture and even in our everyday speech. Because so many people searched for so many years and never found El Dorado, the name has come to symbolize a lifelong quest for an often-impossible dream. Sometimes these obsessive searches involve mythical objects, like the Holy Grail, but at other times they're about abstract concepts like youth, wealth, love, or happiness. Many towns and cities are also named after El Dorado, and true to their namesake, whatever gold they're hiding has remained hidden!

There can be little doubt that, despite the countless and varied attempts hunting through the jungle, the Conquistadors never uncovered all the secrets of the Amazon. Biology, botany, and anthropology show us that there is still plenty of potential for new discoveries. Did the Spanish adventurers really find the lake of El Dorado? Almost certainly Lake Guatavita is that fabled lagoon. But nobody has yet found Manoa, and if the El Dorado myth is ever proven, there is good reason to suspect the Manoan legend will be uncovered, too.

► ESP AND PSYCHOKINESIS ◄

Extrasensory perception (ESP) and psychokinesis (PK) are the two powers that govern all self-controlled human mysteries. ESP is the ability to feel or understand events which are not apparent to the standard five senses, and psychokinesis is a natural force that can be used to physically affect the world without any physical contact. Together, these two talents are known as psychic powers or psi, and some researchers believe they are inherent in us all. Other scientists think they are nothing but hoaxes or magic tricks that have never been proven in controlled laboratory conditions.

The idea of ESP has been around for centuries. Animals are known to have instincts and senses that are inexplicable if we rely purely on the five established receptors. For example, trained dogs can feel when an epileptic person will have a fit, and can give the sufferer warning so that they can take medication and safety precautions. Advocates of human ESP suggest that we are born with similar powers, but that our comfortable modern lifestyles have allowed these natural powers to atrophy.

The first scientifically tested experiments to investigate the subject of ESP were conducted by Joseph Banks Rhine in the 1930s. Rhine was a scientist at Duke University in Durham, North Carolina, and developed the now-archetypal ESP-testing, card guessing game. Rhine would ask the subjects in his experiments which one of five cards he was holding—the card would either show a circle, a square, a plus sign, a star, or three wavy lines. The pack contained 25 cards, and the success rate of the subject compared to the pure statistics of probability indicated whether some external, unknown sense might be at play.

Rhine concluded that ESP was a genuine phenomenon that could be affected by the person involved in the experiment. He discovered that if people were relaxed and comfortable, their success rate would improve, but if those being tested were bored, scared, or simply disliked the notion of ESP, their results would actually be worse than probability.

Character and situation are said to have great bearing on individual ESP sensitivity. Particularly stressful or traumatic scenarios are believed to encourage much more receptivity to instinctive senses. Those who call themselves psychics are said to be naturally in tune with their inherent powers, and can feel unexplained sensations as easily as normal people receive the known five.

Many researchers, who utterly disbelieve the notion of psi, point to the long history of so-called psychics being revealed as charlatans, con men, or illusionists. Similarly, they question every aspect of the controlled experiments used to prove the existence of ESP and point to the fact that the "successful" tests are often unrepeatable. Some scientists have asked why it is that, if brainwaves exist, we can't build a machine to detect them? It can also be argued that ESP tests can appear to be successful by the simple effect of good luck, whereas psychokinetic experiments are far less susceptible to chance. People involved in psychokinetic experiments can either make things move psychically or they can't.

Needless to say, the public does not understand psychokinetic energy very well, because there have not been any substantially successful tests. The evidence that we do have comes purely from anecdotes. That said, the phenomenon of poltergeists is well documented—if not laboratory tested—and is believed to contain a great deal of psychokinetic influence.

Certainly, many traditional biologists and physicists would refute the existence of any forces that are not explained by science. When such phenomena are reinforced by unconvincing evidence, their credibility is questioned further. However, the public perception of psi ability is quite different, and recent surveys have shown that two-thirds of American adults believe they have experienced some occurrence of ESP. In many ways, the subject is akin to the question of God, or the human soul. Are there actually forces we can feel and control, but that our intelligence cannot yet understand?

TOP TEN REAL-LIFE PSYCHICS:

* Oracle at Delphi: Priestess who prophesied in ancient Greece.
* Isaiah: Biblical prophet.
* Nostradamus: Foretold major events with cryptic verses.
* Daniel Douglas Home: Held séances that featured levitation.
* Edgar Cayce: Diagnosed illnesses in a trance.
* Uri Gellar: Stunningly psychokinetic stage performer.
* Dr. Doreen Virtue: Helps people communicate with angels.
* Sylvia Browne: Media personality and medium who helps police locate criminals.
* John Edwards: Helps TV audience members communicate with dead family members.
* Miss Cleo: Hosted a psychic phone hotline. Charged with deceptive practices.

► THE GREAT FLOOD ◄

Jesus Christ himself referred to the Great Flood but Christians aren't the only ones who believe in the story. The Torah offers accounts of the disaster, and it is also referenced in the Koran. The first historical record of the disaster appeared in eighteenth century BCE Babylonian writings, and the ancient *Epic of Gilgamesh* also describes a great flood. Flood references exist in hundreds of cultures around the world; ancient Greeks, Romans, and Native Americans all have tales of a terrible flood that left few survivors. There are suggestions that the flood of Noah, described in the Bible, may have been the same event that destroyed Atlantis. Although tradition and mythology provide strong circumstantial evidence, recent scientific knowledge has given actual support to the Great Flood theory.

In the 1990s, two geologists from Columbia University, William Ryan and Walter Pitman, pieced together clues that they believed suggested a great ancient flood actually did occur. Ryan and Pitman formulated a theory proposing that the European ice sheets melted about 7,500 years ago as the world grew warmer following the

Noah should get a place in the **Guinness Book of World Records** for World's Biggest Houseboat.

DID YOU KNOW...THE MYTH IS PRACTICALLY UNIVERSAL?

Hundreds of cultures have stories about an ancient, massive flood that nearly wiped out their civilizations. Many of these myths share common elements, including: A deity causing the flood to wipe out evil in the world, people escaping to a mountain or waiting it out on a floating vessel, birds being sent out to see if the waters had subsided, a rainbow indicating the end of the disaster, and a single family being the only survivors. No word on how the families reacted to being cooped up together for so long.

last Ice Age. The excess water caused the Mediterranean to overflow into the Black Sea, which Ryan and Pitman believe was initially a shallow, landlocked freshwater lake with river-fed fertile plains surrounding it. They suggest that it was a heavily populated area that was submerged by rising sea levels.

Ryan and Pitman suggested that as the ice melted, the Black Sea rose by as much as six inches per day, with water rushing in at 200 times the rate of Niagara Falls. Within a year, 60,000 square miles of land were lost under water, and the fresh water basin became a saltwater extension of the ocean. Rising water levels and loss of freshwater resources forced away farmers and settlers who had relied on the area's natural environment. Ryan and Pitman believe the ancient lake's shoreline now lies around 5,000 feet below the present water level. Sediment core samples from the center of the Black Sea contain plant roots and mud cracks, which suggest a dry riverbed covered in a layer of mud, indicating a great flood.

In 1999, the underwater explorer Robert Ballard, who had previously discovered remains of the Titanic, also studied the area. He and his team found a previous coastline 550 feet deep and 20 miles out into the Black Sea. They took samples, which included freshwater and saltwater mollusks, from the ancient seabed. Apart from the well-preserved geographical and oceanographic features of the underwater area, which pointed to a coastline flooding gradually, the freshwater mollusk species were carbon-dated at an age older than the saltwater mollusks. Scientists also discovered that the freshwater mollusks all seemed to die at the same time, suggesting an immediate change in environment. The youngest freshwater shells were found to be 7,460 years old, whereas the oldest saltwater creatures were around 6,820 years old. This suggests the flood happened somewhere between those two dates, confirming Ryan and Pitman's original theory.

Evidence from the bottom of the Black Sea proves it was once dry land. So the questions is: Was it drowned during Noah's flood?

Ballard returned to the area in September 2000 and discovered even more fascinating revelations. His team found ancient tools and rubbish sites, and crucially, what may be a prehistoric dwelling. The wooden-beamed man-made structure, found 300 feet down, contained ceramic vessels and stone tools. The team referred to it as "Noah's House," although radiocarbon dating has proved it was too young to be from Noah's time. However, it did provide real evidence that the area was inhabited before the Great Flood and that there would have been witnesses to the catastrophic event. The condition of the house also showed that the flood had happened at such a speed that surface waves did not have time to batter the building before consuming it.

These discoveries offer many avenues for further study. Anthropologists research the effect of disasters on population movements, and how ancient races have passed on their stories by word of mouth. Geologists and oceanographers study immense sea level changes and flood lands, particularly with the looming threat of global warming. For scholars, historians, and the religious alike, the confirmation of an amazing biblical story is a welcome change in an age of legend-destroying scientific discovery. Sometimes even the oldest stories hold startlingly new revelations.

► THE GREAT PYRAMID AT GIZA ◄

The Ancient Egyptians believed that after mortal death the soul or spirit would continue life in another dimension. They buried their Pharaoh kings, whom they regarded as living gods, with all the treasures and objects needed to survive in comfort in the afterlife. They also embalmed the bodies to ensure that the mortal remains would be mummified and preserved for whatever fate awaited the kings. Most importantly, they built impressive burial structures to demonstrate the dead person's importance and to aid that person's ascendancy to the next dimension in the heavens. The most famous and mysterious of these buildings are Egypt's pyramids, and the most mystical of these is the Great Pyramid of Cheops at Giza. However, many people question whether the structure really is just a tomb or if the design holds great secrets of civilization.

The pyramids were erected between 2800 BCE and 2200 BCE. The first was built by King Zoser in Saqqara near Memphis. Although the structure was created with six stepped tiers, and is not a strict pyramid as such, it was the first building designed exclusively to house the property and remains of the king. In the following centuries, King Seneferu built his own trio of pyramids. One at Maidum was called the False Pyramid because it was abandoned mid-project due to a structural weakness. One at Dahshur was known as the Bent Pyramid because of a design problem: The gradient of its sides had to be reduced as it was constructed. The final one, the Northern Pyramid of Seneferu, was built close to the Bent Pyramid, and is considered the first true pyramid.

The most impressive structure, however, was completed around 2500 BCE for King Cheops in Giza, ten miles south of the city we now

The pyramids still look pretty good, but the lack of windows is a real killer for potential homebuyers.

The second most well known Egyptian burial structure is the tomb of the pharaoh Tutankhamun—a.k.a. "King Tut." Archaeologist Howard Carter and his team famously discovered the tomb, practically unopened, in 1922. Rumors of a curse circulated, however, when several people associated with the discovery died under strange circumstances. Explanations range from fungal spores to poison placed inside the tomb to deter grave robbers. However, since few of the people died immediately, their illnesses may have been caused by something more…inexplicable.

know as Cairo. The Great Pyramid used an estimated 4,000 builders, tens of thousands more manual laborers, and stands 481 feet high. It may have taken up to 30 years to quarry and assemble the two and a half million blocks of limestone used, which weigh over six and a half million tons. The base of the pyramid covers an area of just over 30 acres. Its builders lavished great care on Cheops's structure, and although later pyramids were built nearby for King Chephren and King Mycerinus, neither is of the same quality.

The Great Pyramid's sides run perfectly north to south and east to west to within a tenth of a degree. The base is an almost exact square, with an error margin of just seven inches, while the pavement around the structure is level to within an inch. Unlike other pyramids, this one houses a great number of chambers and corridors, with an ascending passageway that runs directly north for 345 feet. Oddly, Caliph Abdullah al Mamun found nothing inside the structure when he first opened it in 820 CE, though it had been widely assumed that the pyramid stood as a great monument to hold the body and treasures of King Cheops. Al Mamun and his men circumvented the three huge granite plugs they found blocking the king's chamber, but when they arrived in the great room, they found only an empty stone sarcophagus. So what was the pyramid intended for, if not to house the body of the Cheops? Many fantastical theories have arisen in the absence of evidence for burial ceremonies. Some people believe it was built by God as a stone version of the Bible, or as a record containing references to all events past, present, and future. They believe the various passageways represent historical timelines, and intersections between them mark great happenings, including the birth of Christ and the two World Wars. Some advocates of this theory said it also showed a Second Coming in 1881 and the end of the world in 1953. Other mathematical studies of the Great Pyramid claim that it demonstrates knowledge of the true value of pi, and was built using the "sacred inch."

Another popular theory, from the latter part of the last century indicates that alien visitors constructed the Great Pyramid. The theory proposes that these aliens did everything from creating mankind, to erecting the pyramid as a landing beacon for their next visit to Earth. Another well-known idea, the Orion Theory, was created by Robert Bauval and Adrian Gilbert. They believe the pyramids at Giza are an earthly representation of the three stars in the Orion Nebula. They say the shafts found in the Great Pyramid correlate with important astronomical features visible at the time of the building's construction. The Orion Theory states that the Ancient Egyptians descended directly from alien visitors, and retained some of their knowledge. These important design features in the Egyptians' tombs were meant to help point the spirits of the dead back toward the celestial bodies they came from.

Does the layout of the pyramids really reflect the position of the stars?

Many of these "ancient astronaut" theories suggest that the pyramids were built around 10,000 years ago, rather than 5,000, as historians commonly believe. Other theories state that the instigating race may not have been aliens, but a now-lost civilization. Psychic and writer Edgar Cayce was convinced that the pyramids were built around 10,000 BCE by travelers from Atlantis. However, his assertion that the Atlanteans also recorded the Second Coming of Christ in 1998 in the design of the pyramid is somewhat flawed. Some theories even suggest that our conception of the chronology of the pyramids is wrong. Some people believe the build quality of the pyramids actually deteriorated rather than improved, as the initial knowledge brought by the instigating race was lost over time.

Although the Great Pyramid has been explored and studied more than any other ancient structure in Egypt, scientists are constantly making new discoveries. In 1954 a previously unknown sealed pit was found on the south side, containing a 140-foot-long cedar boat, which may have been buried to help the king travel to the afterlife. In recent years, space equipment and remote-controlled probes have been used to examine the building in new ways. However, conspiracy theories and tales of hidden secrets have only increased, since NASA has refused to publish underground readings taken by the space shuttle, and the Egyptian government has been reluctant to encourage deeper exploration. For the world's interested public, the mystery of the Great Pyramid at Giza is as unknown today as when Caliph Abdullah al Mamun first reopened it over a millennium ago.

▶ THE HOLY GRAIL ◀

Almost everything we know about the Holy Grail is derived from the romantic Arthurian tales of the twelfth and thirteenth centuries. However, there are some generally accepted details: The Grail is believed to be the chalice of the Eucharist, or dish of the Pascal lamb, used by Jesus at the Last Supper. According to the Gospels, this vessel was taken by Joseph of Arimathea, a secret disciple of Jesus, who used it to collect blood from the crucified body of Jesus. An alternative theory held by some Christians is that it was a chalice given to Joseph by Jesus Christ in a vision. This vessel's holy powers sustained Joseph for 42 years during his incarceration by the Jews. In either case, Joseph brought the holy chalice to Britain, thus beginning the true legend.

Some people believe the Holy Grail was secretly passed down through generations of Joseph's descendants. Others believe it is buried in the Chalice Well at Britain's oldest holy city, Glastonbury, which indicates a connection to Arthurian legend. Romantic tales say that Arthur and his Knights of the Round Table set off on a holy quest to find the Grail. A more reliable legend says the Cathars, a medieval Christian sect, had possession of the Grail and hid it in the Pyrenees before they were overrun.

It has been suggested that they may have kept it at their stronghold of Montségur, which was actually searched by Nazi forces looking for the Grail during World War II. Others believe the Cathars hid it at

The legend of the Holy Grail has changed over the centuries—but it's never strayed too far from the central idea of death.

Rennes-le-Château, or gave the chalice to the Knights Templar for safekeeping. Some researchers believe a field in Shropshire hides the Grail under its surface, and another tradition states that a wooden cup in a Welsh country house is the true artifact. Valencia Cathedral, in Spain, holds a chalice that many believe is the actual cup used by Jesus at the Last Supper. It has been used by many popes, including Pope Benedict XVI in 2006. The organized Church does not credit any legend, although that should not be seen as any indication that it is purely a myth.

From medieval texts, to *Monty Python*, to the *Indiana Jones* movies, there are numerous versions of the "grail quest," or search for the grail. In several of the stories, knights and other seekers must prove themselves worthy, or find some greater truth inside themselves, before reaching the grail. In most versions the grail is portrayed as a cup, but it has also been referred to as a dish, a saucer, and a bowl. Whether any hard evidence of the fabled chalice's existence is ever found or not, the story of the Holy Grail will continue to puzzle us for many years to come.

DID YOU KNOW...THE GRAIL MAY NOT HAVE BEEN A CUP AT ALL?

According to one theory, found in the novel *The Da Vinci Code*, the so-called Holy Grail was actually the person of Mary Magdalene, who had a relationship with Jesus and carried his child. According to this way of thinking, Mary was herself the vessel that carried the bloodline of Jesus. To find the grail is to find the grave—and the remains—of Mary Magdalene. Some believe that the bloodline of Jesus and Mary Magdalene still exists today. We'll never know the truth until someone finds the grail—but figuring out whether the grail is literal or metaphorical only adds another layer of mystery to the story.

► JACK THE RIPPER ◄

In 1888, the world's most famous serial killer stalked the dark, grimy streets of Victorian London's East End. Jack the Ripper was the original celebrity mass murderer. The fear surrounding the Zodiac Killer in the 1960s and '70s, for example, held many similarities with the terror created by this forefather of death-dealing criminals. In these types of cases, the impact of the crimes is heightened by the mystery surrounding the killer's identity. Unlike many of his modern counterparts, Jack the Ripper was never caught or even named. To this day it has never been conclusively proven who he really was.

London's Whitechapel district was known as one of the poorest areas of the city, and was home to over a thousand prostitutes. The Ripper's reign of terror officially began in the opening hours of August 31, 1888, when a market porter spotted a woman lying in a doorway on Buck's Row in Whitechapel. Rather than approach the woman, the porter went to find the beat policeman, who found that the woman's throat had been deeply cut. A medical examination later revealed her body had been mutilated. She was identified as Mary Ann "Polly" Nichols, a 42-year-old prostitute.

Barely a week later, at 6 am on September 8, the body of another woman was found in Hanbury Street, near Buck's Row. She was Annie Chapman, a 45-year-old prostitute whose head had been almost entirely severed from her neck. She had also been disemboweled.

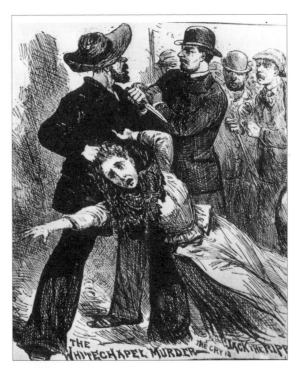

Jack the Ripper strikes again in this (admittedly pretty frightening) illustration from the time.

Fear was beginning to spread throughout the community. For the first time in history, the people had a literate public and a scrutinizing press who were putting the police under a new sort of pressure. Not only were the police there to protect the people of London, they also had to cope with the novel stress of proving their own competence. Just as in modern mass murder cases, the effect of supposition, myths, and rumors in newspaper coverage led to a great deal of anxiety.

By the time the Ripper struck again, the murders were the most talked-about event in the Whitechapel area. In the early hours of September 30, a costume jewelry salesman arrived home on Berners Street, where he discovered the body of Elizabeth Stride, a prostitute whose throat had been slit. As police rushed to the scene and searched the nearby streets, the Ripper made off to Mitre Square, in the City of London, and killed Catharine Eddowes. Although the earlier victim had not been mutilated, many believe the Ripper had been interrupted during the second procedure. Eddowes's remains were not as well-preserved—she was found disemboweled.

This night become known as the "double event," and was the subject of many letters sent in to the police. Although most came from members of the public offering advice, some were purported to have come from the Ripper himself. Some were given more credence than others. One letter, dated September 28, goaded and teased the police. It was the origin of the name Jack the Ripper, which was how the sender signed off. The second was a postcard dated October 1 that referred to the double event. The third letter was posted two weeks later and included a section of a kidney allegedly removed from Catharine Eddowes. Although the police could not rule out that these correspondences came from a crank or a hoaxer, the kidney

DID YOU KNOW...THE LONDON POLICE MAY HAVE INVENTED SNEAKERS?

The police investigating the Jack the Ripper murders had a difficult task. They had little experience with serial murders, and there were no forensics procedures in the late 1800s. One of the few things they could do was try to catch the killer in the act. In desperation, they attached strips of rubber to the bottoms of their boots, in an attempt to try and sneak up on the killer silently. Though rubber-soled shoes called plimsolls were manufactured in the 1830s, the first sneakers weren't produced until after the murders, in 1892.

included in the third letter was shriveled and diseased. Not only was Eddowes an alcoholic, but she also suffered from Bright's disease (a chronic kidney disease), and this organ displayed all the signs of these afflictions.

The next—and final— murder attributed to Jack the Ripper occurred on November 9 in Miller's Court, a site close to the other murders. Another prostitute, 24-year-old Mary Jane Kelly, was found by her landlord— Kelly's body was utterly mutilated. This time, the murder had taken place inside, and the killer had had all night to dissect the corpse.

There is the possibility that the Ripper may have killed two or three more women in London around this time. However, the police were unable to find the perpetrator of the crimes and suppressed information to try to reassure the public. Despite this, Londoners were fully aware that police work was proving fruitless at determining the Ripper's identity. The police had their theories, however. Police doctors who examined the bodies suggested the Ripper had had medical training. In 1894 the Chief Constable of the Metropolitan Police Force, Sir Melville Macnaghten, wrote a report that named Montague John Druitt, a barrister who committed suicide shortly after the Kelly murder, as the most likely suspect. However, the

time Macnaghten believed Druitt to be a trained doctor, a fact subsequent research proved false.

Annie Chapman, a victim of the Ripper.

Macnaghten also named two more possible suspects. One was Aaron Kosminski, a man who lived in the Whitechapel area and was placed in an insane asylum in March 1889. Although one of the chief investigating officers, Robert Anderson, believed he was guilty, nothing from Kosminski's asylum records suggests he was homicidal. Macnaghten's final suspect, Michael Ostrog, from Russia, had a psychiatric disorder. Despite being a convicted criminal and possibly having some medical training, his behavior under studied conditions also did not indicate an ability for multiple murders. In recent years, investigators have considered Dr. Francis Tumblety, an American doctor who fled London shortly after the murders. Despite thinking him a possible suspect, the police at the time decided to rule him out.

As with many mysteries, the Ripper's identity has attracted conspiracy theorists. People from all walks of life—royalty, royal servants, high-ranking police officers, Russian spies, and even crazed evangelists—have been considered as the killer. More recently, the crime writer Patricia Cornwell conducted her own study. She used $4 million of her own money to investigate a possible link between the Ripper and Walter Sickert, an impressionist painter who may have had connections with Whitechapel around the time of the murders. Twenty years after the killings, he created a series of paintings that depicted dead and gruesomely mauled prostitutes. Cornwell's controversial 2002 book, *Portrait of a Killer*, argues for Sickert's guilt.

Modern Ripper investigators, like the Victorian London police, fail to agree with each other. There are many suspects that could have been linked to the murders in some way. As the years blur the truth, so the plausibility of many different suspects increases, while the definitive proof needed disappears in the fog of time.

► KASPAR HAUSER ◄

On May 26, 1828, a teenage boy stumbled up to the gates of Nuremberg. He had a strong build, light curly hair, a pale complexion, and moved as if he was drunk. A local shoemaker, Georg Weickmann, approached the boy to see who he was, but the lad only said, "I would like to be a rider the way my father was." He handed Weickmann an envelope addressed to the captain of the fourth squadron of the 6th regiment of the Light Cavalry. The shoemaker took him to the captain, who opened the letter. It explained that the boy had been left with a poor laborer who had kept him locked inside all his life, but the boy was now ready to serve in the king's army.

The cavalry captain questioned the boy, but all he would say was, "don't know," "take me home," and "horse." He could also write the name "Kaspar Hauser." Finally, the captain put the boy in the local prison where the jailer took pity on him. The jailer's children began to teach him to speak, write, and draw. He seemed to have no concept of normal human behavior as he had no facial expressions, could not understand the difference between men and women, was happy to sleep sitting up, acted like a baby or infant child, and was particularly happy in the dark.

In July 1828, a local magistrate suggested to Nuremberg's authorities that it would be best for Hauser to be taken out of the jail and placed in the custody of George Friedrich Daumer, a university professor and psychologist. Daumer tried to help socialize Hauser, but also kept a record of the boy's strange behavior. Daumer was amazed by Hauser's heightened senses. He could read in the dark, hear whispers from extreme distances, and discern who was in a pitch black room simply by their smell.

SPOTLIGHT ON...FERAL CHILDREN

Feral children are those raised in the wilderness without human contact, often with animal families. Though they might seem fictional—and though many such famous fictional characters have been created, including Mowgli, Peter Pan, and Tarzan—there have been numerous reported cases throughout history, and several in the twenty-first century. Feral children lack basic social skills, and may have trouble speaking, relating to humans, and using common items, such as kitchen utensils. Instead they may act more like the animals they once lived with. Though Kaspar Hauser had similar characteristics, he was not technically a feral child, and was able function in society (sort of).

However, as his awareness and education about the world around him increased, these extraordinary abilities waned.

By early 1829, Hauser had learned enough to be able to write his autobiography. In it he revealed that he had been kept in a cell seven feet long, four feet wide, and five feet high by a man whose face he never saw. He slept on a straw bed, and when he woke there would be water and bread for him to eat. Sometimes the water would taste odd, and he would pass out only to find himself cleaned and groomed, and wearing a fresh set of clothes when he woke. One day the man came to Hauser's cell with books and taught him to read a little, write his name, and pronounce the rudimentary phrases he had repeated on his public arrival. The following day, Hauser and his captor began a three-day journey which culminated in his appearance at Nuremberg.

Hauser's autobiography opened the door to a new terror. In October 1829, a stranger dressed in black came to Daumer's house and tried to kill Hauser with a knife. Lord Stanhope, an English aristocrat and friend of the ruling Baden family, then struck up a friendship with Hauser, and gained guardianship of the boy. Stanhope quickly lost interest of Hauser, however, and placed the boy in the town of Ansbach under the care of a man named Dr. Meyer. Meyer disliked the boy and became a hard and mean-spirited tutor. On December 14, 1831, Hauser went to a local park to meet a man who had promised to reveal details about his mother's identity. They met, and the stranger motioned as if to give Hauser a wallet, but as the young man leaned forward, he was stabbed in his side. He died three days later, at the young age of 21.

The suspicion developed that Hauser was actually a Baden prince and son of Stephanie, Grand Duchess of Bavaria. Certainly many of the Bavarian aristocracy had such suspicions, and King Ludwig of Bavaria even wrote in his diary that Hauser was the "rightful Grand Duke of Baden." The theory is that Stephanie and Karl of Baden had Hauser in 1812, but Karl's stepmother, the Duchess of Hochberg, switched him at birth with a sickly peasant child. The ill baby soon passed away and subsequent boys sired by Karl with Stephanie also died young. Karl himself died in strange circumstances, and on his deathbed said he believed that he and his boys had been poisoned. Karl's throne then went to his stepbrother, the Duchess of Hochberg's son, Leopold. It is an unprovable theory.

All we definitely know is that in a peaceful countryside churchyard there is a gravestone that reads:

"Here lies Kaspar Hauser, riddle of his time. His birth was unknown, his death mysterious."

► KING ARTHUR ◄

The legend of King Arthur states that he was born at some time during the fifth century. It is said that the great magician Merlin disguised Uther Pendragon, one of Britain's great warriors, to look like the Duke of Tintagel, the husband of Ingraine of Cornwall. Uther seduced Ingraine at Tintagel cottage, and the child they conceived was given away at birth. He was named Arthur and was raised completely unaware of his special lineage. When Uther died, the throne was empty.

Merlin set a sword called Excalibur in rock and stated that only someone of a truly royal bloodline would be able to remove Excalibur from its fixed position. When the young Arthur was the only one able to do this, he was pronounced king. Eleven other British rulers rebelled against the young leader, but Arthur quashed their uprising and began a noble and glorious reign.

Arthur married Guinevere and assembled a group of courageous and honest knights at a kingdom seat in Camelot, in the Vale of Avalon. To avoid any sense of preference among the knights, Guinevere's father provided Arthur with the fabled Round Table. Together, Arthur and his knights had great victories over both Saxon invaders and the Roman Empire. Arthur is even said to have become emperor himself, and set about on a search for the Holy Grail. However, during this time one of Arthur's most trusted knights, Lancelot, had an affair with Guinevere.

This marked the beginning of the end for Arthur. The two lovers fled to Lancelot's land in Brittany, France. Arthur decided to follow and wage war on his former friend, leaving his nephew Mordred as custodian of England. While he was battling across the English Channel, Mordred rebelled, and Arthur was forced to return home. A fierce

SPOTLIGHT ON...THE HOLY GRAIL

According to legend, the search for the Holy Grail—either the cup that Jesus used at the Last Supper, or the one that caught his blood during his crucifixion—was critical for King Arthur and his knights. The Grail was hidden away in a castle and guarded by a man known as the Fisher King, who had a fatal injury. If the Grail was found, the wastelands surrounding the castle would be restored, and the Fisher King would be healed. The most important outcome, however, would be the knights overcoming adversity and finding their best selves during the quest.

battle ensued on Salisbury Plain. Arthur managed to kill Mordred, but the king himself was also mortally wounded. On the brink of death, he returned to Avalon. He is said to have thrown Excalibur into the kingdom's lake and then he disappeared into a cave, pledging he would return if danger ever threatened England.

The first historical proof we have of an Arthurian-type figure is in Gildas's sixth century *De Excidio Britanniae* which refers to British soldiers being led by a man called Ambrosius Aurelianus. The name Arthur appears in Nennius's ninth century *Historia Brittonum*. However, it was not until the twelfth century that the phenomenon of Arthur as an historical icon really had an impact. William of Malmesbury and Geoffrey of Monmouth produced works that sowed the seeds of the Arthurian legend. Unfortunately, their works also included many fictional details that have subsequently obscured the true reality of Arthur's reign.

There is other evidence for his place in historical fact. Many people believe that Glastonbury in Somerset is the true site of Camelot, and in the twelfth century it was claimed that Arthur's grave had been found there. Similarly, the Isles of Scilly are said to host the remains of the great king. Certainly there are plenty of candidates for places featured in Arthurian mythology, and historians have discovered many historical figures who could have actually been the king. Historians believe that the sheer number of possibilities as to Arthur's true identity is probably the reason that our knowledge has become so blurred— that the identity of Arthur is the result of confusion among, or is the amalgamation of many individual personal histories.

What we do know is that in the sixth century many Celtic realms had leaders born who were called Arthur and this could have been in homage to the original king. Although the use of the name has clouded the original Arthur's legend, it also points to the fact that a truly great and inspirational leader was present a generation before.

Perhaps the most remarkable evidence has only surfaced in recent years. In July 1998, archaeologists found a slab marked in Latin with the name "Artagnov" or "Arthnou" on a rocky hilltop in Tintagel, Cornwall. The slab dates to the sixth century, and proves that the name was present in the legendary Arthurian lands at the correct time, and belonged to a man of some standing. We may never know exactly who the legend of King Arthur represents, but with more finds like this, we can only move closer to the truth.

▶ THE KNIGHTS TEMPLAR ◀

A group of nine French knights founded an order in Jerusalem in 1118 under the title The Poor Fellow-Soldiers of Christ. The warriors took monastic vows and pledged their lives to protecting Christian travelers and the Holy Land. They were housed at the palace of King Baldwin II, the French King of Jerusalem, on the site of Solomon's Temple, which is how they gained their title, the Knights Templar. In 1128 they were officially sanctioned by Pope Honorius II, and provided with a "Rule" from Saint Bernard of Clairvaux. The knights gained a fearsome reputation for being courageous, honorable, and ferocious in battle. They fought in the Crusades alongside Richard the Lionheart and accumulated incredible gifts from grateful European monarchs.

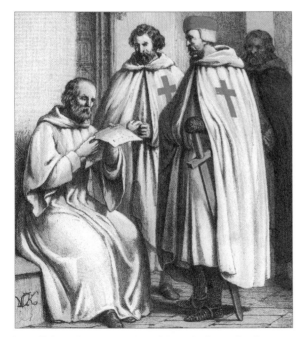

Some Knights Templar read aloud from the latest Dan Brown bestseller.

Within 200 years the Templars had left the Holy Land for Paris, but such was their influence that they were only required to answer to the Pope. Their riches were so immense that they began the earliest form of organized banking, and lent money to European monarchies. But this, combined with a history of holding meetings in secret, led to their downfall. King Philip the Fair of France was known to owe staggering sums to the order. On October 13, 1307, he announced that the Templars had engaged in heretical activities at their meetings, arrested all members of the order in France, and seized their assets. The Templars accepted his decision, but many were still tortured into giving false confessions of unholy practices. However, only the Pope could condemn the monks, and a newly installed Pope Clement V was happy to bow to Philip's coercions.

The order was disbanded, and it was suggested that all European monarchies take whatever steps were necessary to ensure that the order would never recover. On March 19, 1314, the last Grand Master of the Knights Templar, Jacques de Molay, was burned at the stake on an island in the middle of the River Seine in Paris. As the flames rose, it is claimed de Molay cursed King Philip and the Pope, threatening that they would both follow him within a year. And in fact, they did—Clement died a month later and Philip seven months after that. It is said that de Molay

FUN FACTS:
TEMPLAR MYTH VS. FACT

Myth: Many think the association of Friday the 13th with bad luck comes from the date that King Philip arrested the French Templars, but that's actually a modern myth.

Myth: The Templars did not actually have massive wealth. They took vows of poverty and only accumulated what people gave them.

Fact: In addition to inventing banking, the knights also invented checks.

TBD: One theory says that instead of hiding their treasure in Scotland, they may have taken off for the New World and hidden it in Canada.

passed on his powers to a successor before his death, but the movement did not emerge again until 1705. During the intervening years, some of the Templars are believed to have taken refuge in Scotland.

Since then the order has had associations with Freemasonry and other secret societies, and it has flourished with many high-profile and influential members. Recently, following World War II, the cohesion of the international order has become somewhat fractured. The meetings are still held in secret.

Apart from fiercely guarded rituals and traditions, it would seem that there are few mysteries surrounding the order. But one question remains: Why didn't the Parisian Templars fight when arrested by Philip's men? In the days leading up to their capture, a heavily laden cart was supposedly removed from their buildings. Philip never found all the riches in their offices that he wished to acquire, and it seems the knights submitted to his thuggery meekly, in order to let their great treasure escape. So what was this treasure? The obvious theory is that it was gold and jewels taken from holy temples of Jerusalem and the biblical world during the Crusades. However, many have speculated that the reaction of the Templars suggested that it was something beyond material value, and may have been something of enormous spiritual importance, such as the Ark of the Covenant or the Holy Grail. Others have considered that it may be secret Christian knowledge, such as the truth about the bloodline of Jesus Christ.

The treasure, whatever nature it takes, has never been found, and where it is hidden remains a mystery. Many Templar experts think it may have been the root of Bérenger Saunière's mysterious wealth, and believe it was buried at the church of Rennes-le-Château. However, one of the most widely held theories is that the surviving Templars hid it at Rosslyn Chapel in Scotland. If the order did manage to continue throughout its banished years, there is good reason to believe the secrets of the treasure are known to only a select few. To the rest of us, members of the Knights Templar are only modern day descendants of a historical mystery.

If you got it, flaunt it, Knights!

► LEVITATION ◄

Many people famous for their levitation abilities have had fervent and passionate states of mind. The early Christian church believed levitation was a sign of demonic possession. However, throughout the centuries, many holy people have also appeared to lift themselves off the ground. The most famous was probably St Joseph of Copertino, born in 1603 in Apulia, Italy, who reached a state of religious ecstasy that apparently allowed him to defy gravity. He is said to have levitated over a hundred times in his life, and it was the demonstration of his rapture-induced ability in front of Pope Urban VIII that led to his canonization.

Eastern philosophies and religions teach that people can achieve levitation through a devoted study to fully harness the body's life force. This natural energy is called *Ch'i* or *Ki* and is said to be controlled by extensive yogic training. The phenomenon of yogic hops, where a person can make short levitational movements using transcendental meditation, is also advanced by Eastern teachings. Eastern philosophy focuses less on extreme emotion, and more on visualization and breath control to summon up all latent energy within the body.

Some psychics also believe the power needed to levitate ourselves is a naturally inherent psychokinetic power. The nineteenth-century medium Daniel Douglas Home was known as a practiced proponent of the levitating craft. In 1868 he was seen levitating

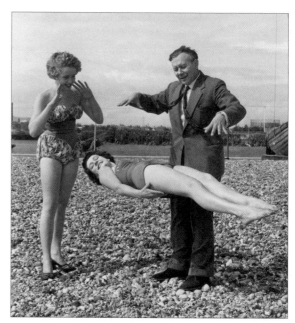

No one's quite clear on when it happened, or why, but somehow bathing suits became the go-to uniform for levitators. (Although they call them "floating suits.")

out of a window on the third story of a building. It was reported that he reentered the building through another window on the same floor. Unlike instances of levitation connected with religion, Douglas Home did not enter a trance. He believed it just required a good deal of concentration. However, many people in the modern age believe levitation is best left to the engineers, designers, and magicians in glamorous cabaret shows.

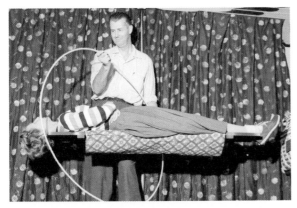

This guy just wants his novelty hula hoop back.

CHRONOLOGY: LEVITATION

Stories of levitation appear throughout history, from ancient times to the present day. Who levitated, you ask? Well, just about everyone. Some well-known cases include:

- Sixth century BCE: The Buddha
- Second century: Christian heretic Simon Magus
- Fourth century: The ancient Greek, Apollonius of Tyana
- Thirteenth century: The Tibetan yogi Milarepa
- Sixteenth century: St. Teresa of Avila
- Nineteenth century: The medium Daniel Dunglas Home
- Twentieth century: South African Clara Germana Cele, under demonic influence
- Twentieth century: Yoda, fictional Jedi master
- Twenty-first century: Stage magician Criss Angel

▶ THE LOCH NESS MONSTER ◀

Of all the mythical beasts in the world, the most famous (and the most frequently hunted) is probably "Nessie," the Loch Ness Monster. She—the beast is usually referred to as female—is often the first phenomenon thought about when the subject of unexplained mysteries is raised. She is an internationally known celebrity who has probably done more for Scottish tourism than any other Scot. There have been Nessie documentaries, TV programs, films, and even cartoons. But although she seems to appear each year to a select few, she has been too shy to debut in a major scientific investigation. So is there really a strange creature, lost in time, lurking at the bottom of Loch Ness?

Loch Ness is a 24-mile long freshwater lake found in the Great Glenn, a massive crevice in the Scottish Highlands. The loch is up to a thousand feet deep and, in places, a mile-and-a-half wide. The first Nessie sighting dates back to 565 CE, when Saint Columba rescued a swimmer from the beast's advances. Experts now generally think that Saint Columba actually encountered a common marine animal that had ended up outside its natural environment. Although the loch continued to be the focus of strange sightings, it was not until the twentieth century that the phenomenon really flourished.

In 1933 the Loch Ness lakeshore road was built. This initiated a flood of sightings and created the Nessie legend. In April 1933, a local couple spotted an enormous animal rolling and playing in the water. They reported what they had seen to the man in charge of salmon stocks in the loch, who then saw the monster himself. He described it as having a six-foot-long neck, a serpentine head and a huge hump. He suggested the creature was about 30 feet long. In July, a

Loch Ness, Scotland. (The potential weekend home of the Plesiosaur.)

FUN FACTS: NESSIE

Nessie is the most famous thing ever to come out of Scotland, according to a 2006 survey—even more famous than Sean Connery, who played James Bond.

* Some believe that global warming was what killed Nessie.

* In 2005, 100 triathlon participants were insured for £1 million (about $1,566,000 US dollars) in case of Loch Ness Monster bites.

* Nessie has been reported to have been seen on Google Earth.

It showed a strange head and neck appearing from the water, but 60 years later it was revealed to be a fake. In April of 1960, an aeronautical engineer named Tim Dinsdale used a 16 mm movie camera to film something moving through the loch. Experts at the Royal Air Force's photographic department have verified that the footage isn't fake and hasn't been tampered with, though it has never been established exactly what is captured on the film. Dinsdale devoted the rest of his life to finding Nessie.

family from London was driving along when they almost crashed into a massive, dark, long-necked animal that strolled across their path and disappeared into the water. Early in 1934 a young veterinary student was riding his motorcycle along the road when he almost struck a creature. He said it had a large bulky body, with flippers, a long neck and a small head.

Many people have tried to capture the creature on film over the years. One Nessie witness took a rather inconclusive photograph of something appearing from the water in 1933. In 1934 a London doctor released a mysterious photograph of the monster to the public.

New sightings have occurred in recent years. In June 1993, a couple on the bank of the loch saw a huge, strange creature lolling about in the water. They said it must have been about 40 feet long, with a giraffe-like neck and very light-brown flesh. A father and son were on their way home later that same evening when they spotted something odd in the water. They told reporters they saw an animal with a neck like a giraffe swimming swiftly away from the shore. The mounting evidence prompted bookmaker William Hill to slash the odds of there really being a Loch Ness Monster from 500:1 to 100:1. Even though a few thousand private individuals say they have seen her, Nessie has always been coy about exposing herself to scientific research teams. The Academy of Applied Science from

Boston, Massachusetts, operated the first extensive expedition in the early 1970s. The project used underwater cameras and sonar equipment to capture images of what resembled an eight-foot-long flipper, a 20-foot long aquatic body, and even a hazy photo of a creature's face. However, a structured sonar sweep of the loch in 1987, named Operation Deepscan, revealed that the portrait picture of Nessie was actually a tree stump. Deepscan did report various, unaccounted-for, large sonar echoes moving about in the extreme depths of the loch.

The first photo of the Loch Ness Monster, which sparked the current "Nessiemania."

Other recent scientific evidence has been more hopeful. A team of Norwegian scientists, the Global Underwater Search Team, picked up bizarre noises in the loch in March 2000. Whatever was making the sounds even crashed into the team's underwater microphone. This group had already recorded unusual sounds from another mythically monster-infested lake in Norway. The noises found in Loch Ness are described as a cross between a snorting horse and a pig eating, and closely match the experiences in Norway. This suggests there are unknown creatures in both lakes, and that they might actually be related. Sonar equipment has more recently discovered huge underwater caverns opening onto the bottom of the loch. These have been called "Nessie's Lair," and may well be large enough to house a whole family of monsters.

It is agreed that a breeding colony of beasts would be needed to continue the existence of such a species, and some witness accounts have reported more than one Nessie appearing on the water's surface. Nessie's actual species is still unknown, although experts

THE LOCH NESS MONSTER

have suggested it may be a manatee or type of primitive whale. It may also be a large otter, a long-necked seal, a huge eel, or even a giant walrus. However, Nessie seems to bear a much stronger resemblance to a creature now thought to be extinct: The plesiosaur, a marine dinosaur that has not been found on Earth for over 60 million years. It had large flippers, a small head, and a large body, and some experts believe a few of these animals were stranded in the loch after the last Ice Age.

None of these suggestions are completely plausible. Even if the plesiosaur did survive the disaster that wiped out the rest of its fellow prehistoric creatures, it is generally believed to be a cold-blooded animal, and would thus not have been able to survive in a chilly Scottish lake. If Nessie is really a modern day aquatic mammal like a whale or a seal, then it would constantly have to come to the surface for air, resulting in many more sightings. With a continued interest that actually grows with each unsuccessful scientific study, this loch remains the home of the world's most mysterious, unexplainable monster.

► LOURDES ◄

On January 7, 1844, Marie Bernarde "Bernadette" Soubirous was born. She was the first child of Francois Soubirous, a poor miller from Lourdes, in southern France, and his wife, Louise. Bernadette was a fragile child, and small in stature. Her father's lack of money meant she was often sent away to be cared for by relatives and friends, and in the summer of 1857 she went to stay with Marie Aravant in the nearby town of Batres. Aravant enjoyed having the girl at her home, but was concerned about her religious development. She tried to teach Bernadette about the Bible, but grew impatient as the teenager failed to show any aptitude for the subject. Finally, Aravant asked a local priest for his advice. He told her to send Bernadette back to Lourdes for Catechism classes.

Shortly after her 14th birthday, the girl arrived back in her hometown. On February 11, 1858, Bernadette was with two friends collecting wood from the shore of the River Gave, west of Lourdes. She decided to walk to a great stone promontory known as *Massabielle*, or the Big Rock, a deserted spot next to the river. A natural hollow 25-feet deep and 40-feet wide was at the base of the cliff. Bernadette heard a noise and looked up. The events that followed would change Bernadette and this area of France forever.

As Bernadette raised her head, she saw a vision of a beautiful lady dressed in white and praying the Rosary. The apparition disappeared but Bernadette returned to the grotto and saw her again. During her third

A portrait of Saint Bernadette of Lourdes. The town has become the destination for hundreds of thousands of Catholic pilgrims every year.

appearance, on February 18, the lady spoke and asked the girl to come to the grotto each day for two weeks. Bernadette did as she was told. One day, the lady told Bernadette to wash herself in the grotto's spring water. There was no spring in the area, so the girl dug into the damp mud and bathed in it. By the next day, a strong spring of fresh water had appeared. During the 13th encounter, the lady asked for a chapel to be built in her honor, and during the 16th appearance the woman revealed her identity as the "Immaculate Conception," which a local priest recognized as a reference to the Virgin Mary. In total,

A CASE IN POINT: LOUIS BOURIETTE

One of the earliest and best-known cures reported at Lourdes is the 1858 case of Louis Bouriette, who lost his sight in a mining accident. A few weeks after the apparitions began, he visited the grotto and prayed, bathing his eye with water from the spring. Shortly after, his blindness was completely cured. Although thousands of people have reported cures, only 67 have been officially recognized by the Catholic Church. Bouriette was one of the lucky ones.

281. LOURDES - Intérieur des Piscines.

Inside the spring at Lourdes. The bearded gentleman on the left does not think too highly of the mustachioed rogue on the floor.

Bernadette saw the Holy Virgin Mother on 18 different occasions, with the last vision occurring on July 16, 1858.

Almost immediately, many of those who drank from or bathed in the grotto's spring reported miraculous cures. In July 1858 the Bishop of Tarbes instigated an investigative commission. For over three-and-a-half years this group of clergymen, doctors, and scientists studied the claims made by Bernadette and worshippers at the grotto. On January 18, 1862, they ruled that Bernadette was an entirely normal girl who really had seen the Virgin Mary. The cures attributed to the spring at Massabielle were declared real, but inexplicable, and the authorities agreed to build a chapel there in homage to the Holy Mother. The chapel has become a major destination for pilgrims.

The main Basilica at Lourdes now comprises three chapels, and there are other churches nearby. The largest, the Basilica of St Pius X, can hold up to 30,000 people—which is useful, since about a million pilgrims visit the site each year. Many travel there to show their respect, or to receive religious solace. Others are critically ill and hope for a cure. In total, there have been nearly 4,000 recoveries from illnesses ranging from tuberculosis, sores, and blindness, to deafness and cancers. A total of 65 miracles attributed to Our Lady of Lourdes have been certified by the Catholic Church.

Bernadette herself was not so lucky. In 1866 she joined the sisters of Nevers at the convent of Saint Gildard. Always frail, she continued to suffer from various illnesses and died on April 16, 1879, at the age of 35. In 1925, Bernadette's perfectly preserved remains were transferred from the convent chapel to a glass casket in the Nevers chapel. It appeared that her body had survived better in death than it had in life. A Doctor Talon, who helped exhume her, later wrote an article for a medical journal saying the state of preservation was not a "natural phenomenon." Bernadette was canonized in 1935, and is now the subject of pilgrimage in her own right.

▶ MEN IN BLACK ◀

The first known encounter with two "men in black" happened in 1947. Two US harbor patrolmen, Harold A. Dahl and Fred L. Crisman, had spotted a UFO over the water of Puget Sound, Washington. Dahl said that a man dressed in black visited him shortly after the sighting and forcefully advised him not to discuss the incident further. A similar meeting happened to Carlo Rossi, from the area near San Pietro a Vico in Italy. In the early hours of July 25, 1952, Rossi was fishing in the River Serchio when he witnessed a strange circular craft hovering over the river. Rossi hid, watching the craft as it first passed over him, then sped away. In the following weeks he told no one about what he had seen, but on September 15 he found a stranger dressed in a dark-blue suit waiting for him by the river. The stranger spoke Italian, but with an odd Scandinavian accent, and had very strange facial features. The man forcefully asked Rossi about what he had seen, but Rossi denied everything.

DID YOU KNOW...THEY AREN'T AS NICE IN REAL LIFE?

The 1997 movie *Men in Black* featured two secret agents monitoring alien activity on Earth, protecting mankind from intergalactic terrorist plots. The Hollywood version portrays these agents as charming folks who advocate for human safety. If the men in black do exist, they seem more concerned with keeping humans—or human memories of UFO encounters—under control. The fictional agents do use one weapon that the real-life men in black would certainly love to have: A device that erases all memory of a men in black encounter. Luckily for us, our memories are the ones that stick.

A bizarre men in black case happened on May 18, 1968, when UFO witnesses started contacting researchers. George Smyth was one of those who had seen a strange object in the skies above Elizabeth, New Jersey. He began to receive visits from strange men, and received phone calls warning him not to attend upcoming UFO conventions or speak to independent investigators. A bizarre aspect of this case was that the three visitors Smyth described were apparently the men he had been told to avoid—the UFO enthusiasts John Keel, Gray Barker, and James Moseley. What made this even more odd was that these three men were actually miles away from Smyth's house at the time of the visits.

Other UFO investigators in the area, John Robinson and his wife, Mary, also noticed strange things happening to them. A large dark car was often parked outside their house in New Jersey, with a strange man inside constantly watching them. One day Mary went out and noticed their friend James Moseley making a spectacle of himself further up the street. She thought this was very strange, but went inside to make a drink for him, thinking he was there to visit them. But then the phone rang. To her surprise it was Moseley, not near her house but at his own home in Manhattan.

More incidents have been reported in recent years. On January 15, 1997, William Shearer experienced a UFO encounter in Essex, southern England. Four days later he heard a knock at the door. Outside stood two strange men, dressed in dark gray suits and long coats. One man stood on guard by a large imposing saloon car, and the other stood at Shearer's threshold. This man was said to be very tall, deathly pale but with bright red lips, and he spoke in a very unusual, almost automated way. He repeatedly asked to come in but Shearer refused and the men finally said they would come back later.

A month later, Shearer was at work when two men appeared. One was the visitor who had stood by the car outside Shearer's house, and the other was a man he'd never seen. They were both dressed in suits with hats, and they told him they wanted to talk about his UFO experience. They gave him exact details of the incident, details that Shearer felt only he should know, and were forceful in their requests. Shearer asked to see their IDs, but the men just kept repeating a formulaic set of questions. In the end, Shearer refused to let them into his place of work and the two men disappeared. However, since then, he has reported blatant tapping activity when using his telephone.

Although no one can be absolutely certain, one theory is that these strange visitors are UFO investigators who belong to a research group that has standardized its uniform. Others say they are actually aliens trying to cover their tracks. Skeptics believe they are pranksters or simply figments of witness's imaginations. In most cases, they claim to be from the CIA or intelligence agencies, and there is a theory that these organizations have been happy to assume such identities in recent years as a ready-made method of intimidation. The other option is, of course, that they are from a secret department of government intelligence, trying to control UFO and alien-related sightings.

▶ NOAH'S ARK ◀

The Bible says that God warned Noah that he was planning to wipe out humankind because there was too much sin in the world. He told Noah that he wanted to save Noah and his family and two of each kind of animal, so that creation could continue after the Great Flood. Noah was instructed to build a large wooden ark 45-feet long, 75-feet wide, and 45-feet high that would house and protect all inside creatures as the waters raged. For 40 days and 40 nights the rain poured and the sea rose until the Earth was completely covered. Both the Bible and the Koran say that the ark came to rest on Mount Ararat as the water subsided, and as a result that's exactly where most ark-hunting has taken place.

The mountain lies in the far eastern corner of Turkey close to its borders with Russia, Iran, and Iraq. The highest peak is just under 17,000 feet high, but the ark itself may lie a little further down, in a chasm called the Ahora Gorge. The Koran indicates that the beached vessel rests on the top of an ice-covered mountain in the middle of this gorge. However, this area isn't very easy to explore, and is only accessible for a couple of months each year. Melting ice and rock falls make the Ahora Gorge particularly treacherous, and rolling mists, hidden glaciers, and altitude difficulties have ended the research expeditions of many adventurers. Historically it has always been a politically unstable region, close to many of the world's violent hotspots, and the Turkish government has frequently discouraged any organized investigations.

Despite this, countless researchers searching for the ark have ventured into the area, and may have discovered proof of a wooden construction locked in the ice caps. Machined and treated timbers have been found in areas completely devoid of natural woodland. In 1876 a British ambassador to Turkey found such remains when climbing Mount Ararat. The timber he discovered had been hand-hewn and fixed with an extremely hard black covering. Almost 80 years later, in 1955, an explorer named Fernand Navarra and his son Rafael discovered some wooden beams in a crevice on the mountain. They took samples of the wood, which have since been carbon dated and identified as roughly 4,000 years old.

Sightings of the ark itself have also been documented. The first modern encounter is said to have happened in 1856 when a group of young English scientists climbed the mountain with two local guides. Despite everyone swearing to keep the discovery secret, two members of the search team independently revealed details on their deathbeds. Around 1910, an official Russian military expedition commissioned by the Tsar claimed to have found Noah's Ark and

took measurements and photographs of the vessel. The results and reports sent back to the Tsar were all lost or destroyed during the Russian Revolution, but many independent witnesses account for the events that occurred. Crucially, everybody who claims to have found the remains has done so in the same area of Mount Ararat.

In more recent years, aerial technology has provided an overall picture of the mountain, and has suggested the ark may lie in a different location. In 1949 a US Air Force mission photographed an unusual feature 15,500 feet up on the northwestern plateau of Mount Ararat on the other side from the Ahora Gorge. The images appear to show the bow of a ship poking out of a glacier. The phenomenon was called the "Ararat Anomaly," and it resurfaced in the 1970s when military satellites were able to focus on the area from space. Since then, more high-powered, clearer commercial satellites have allowed researchers a better chance of examining the strange structure. It seems to be 600 feet long and some experts believe it may be the wooden ribbed structure of an ancient boat.

SPOTLIGHT ON . . .
ALL THOSE ANIMALS

But how did they fit all those animals in there?
Biblical scholars estimate that the Ark had over 100,000 square feet of floor space and over 1.5 million cubic feet in volume—room for 50,000 individual animals. They also believe that at the time there may have been around a million species of animals in existence. Since several of those animals (including many of the insects) lived in or on the water and couldn't survive aboard the ark anyway, it's possible that only 35,000 animals were aboard. One group's verdict? Plenty of room!

Other ark investigators believe it could be simply an old rock formation, an old fortress, or even a crashed airplane. Of course, the only way researchers can gather definite evidence is to be near the site on the ground. But increased tension between Turkey and the area's Kurdish population has hampered exploration attempts, and the recent instability in nearby Iraq has also added to the region's pressures. Until a team of archaeological experts can examine the photographed remains firsthand, the mystery of Noah's Ark will never be solved.

It seems like a mistake to bring the lions along. They don't look very trustworthy.

▶ NOSTRADAMUS ◀

In the modern age, Michel de Nostradamus is associated with one simple notion—prophecies of doom. These prophecies are collected in his great work, *The Centuries,* a collection of around 1,000 four-line verses or quatrains. Nostradamus believed that through his study of astrology, combined with divine guidance, he was able to see the future. He used meditation, mild hallucinogens, and extreme focus to induce his visions. In the first part of *The Centuries,* published in 1555, the verses use a strange and vague language, which Nostradamus claimed he had used purposefully to refute charges of witchcraft. The versus are written in a mixture of French and (less frequently) Latin, Greek, and Italian—and many people who now believe they are able to decipher these verses hail Nostradamus as an accurate predictor of future events. However, the predictions look most accurate in hindsight, with the luxury of fitting real events to suit the text. Few of the predictions made at the end of the twentieth century about the start of the new millennium, which cited his work as reference, have come to pass. So how good a seer was Nostradamus?

Probably the most famous example of Nostradamus's work is the quatrain many enthusiasts say predicted World War II. The text, taken from Century 2, Quatrain 24, in translation reads:

Beasts ferocious from hunger will swim across rivers:

The greater part of the region will be against the Hister,

The great one will cause it to be dragged in an iron cage,

When the Germany child will observe nothing.

Nostradamus believers suggest Hister is Hitler; the "ferocious beasts" are invading Nazis "hungry" for power; and the German nation, "observing nothing," will be imprisoned. The interpretation does have a ring of truth. But skeptics point out that there are no dates given, and terms such as "ferocious beasts," and "the great one" are deeply ambiguous. Also, the Hister is actually a region near the River Danube, so the verse may not refer to Hitler at all. However, other quatrains nearby in the text do seem to mention other important details about the war, and Hitler's personal history shows that he was born near the Danube. So

Michel de Nostradamus, in the flesh.

perhaps, taken as a whole, there is something there.

In recent years, the new millennium and the World Trade Center attack have caused a major reexamination of Nostradamus's work. One of the most talked-about figures in Nostradamus's writings is "Mabus" or "Maddas," who is said to be the next "great evil." In the 1990s, many Nostradamus readers claimed this figure was definitely called Maddas, which is Saddam spelled backward. However, after September 11, 2001, the

spelling became something closer to Mabus, which is an anagram of Usam B, and may refer to Osama, or Usama, bin Laden.

After the World Trade Center attack, a great flood of false Nostradamus verses appeared across the internet. This confused many people, and increased skepticism about his work, even though there are good arguments

TOP 10 NOSTRADAMUS PROPHESIES THAT ACTUALLY CAME TRUE

According to the true believers, Nostradamus correctly predicted the following events (among others), despite the fact that he used vague language and gave no dates for the events:

- ❄ The Great Fire of London
- ❄ The French Revolution
- ❄ The rise of Napoleon
- ❄ Hitler
- ❄ World War II
- ❄ The atomic bombings of Hiroshima and Nagasaki
- ❄ Both Kennedy assassinations
- ❄ The Iraq War
- ❄ Hurricane Katrina
- ❄ The death of Princess Diana
- ❄ The 9/11 attacks

Nostradamus ponders the meaning of it all in his study.

to suggest he predicted the death of John F. Kennedy, the fall of Communism, the French Revolution, and the Challenger Space Shuttle disaster. But the unconvinced refer to the vague language, absence of definite dates, and benefit of back cataloguing events as reasons to doubt. If anybody is interested, he predicts the end of the world in 3797.

Certainly, people of his own period believed in his powers, medical and otherwise. The Queen of France, Catherine de Medici, asked him to plot the horoscope of her husband King Henry II, and in 1564 he was appointed court physician to King Charles IX of France. His final prediction came true on July 2, 1556. The day before, as he left a meeting with his priest, the clergyman allegedly said, "Until tomorrow," to which Nostradamus replied, "You will not find me alive at sunrise." Sure enough, he was dead by morning. It is said that his body is buried with a script which translates his prophecies into more defined predictions. Maybe this script would finally put to rest the debate about just how good a seer Nostradamus really was.

THE OGOPOGO

Wanted criminals often have a reward attached to their heads, but now it seems mythical beasts are also the object of bounty hunters' intentions. Between August 2000 and September 2001 three companies from around Lake Okanegan in British Columbia, Canada, promised $2 million to anyone who could find definitive, living proof that the fabled Ogopogo monster actually existed.

Lake Okanegan is around 100 miles long and has areas almost 1,000 feet deep. The native Salish tribe believed in a terrible serpent, which they called N'ha-a-tik ("Lake Demon"). They said the beast had a cave dwelling near the middle of the lake, and they would often make sacrifices to please the monster. European settlers initially scoffed at the legends, but over the years the Ogopogo has established itself in the minds of many who live nearby.

From the mid-1800s, European immigrants started seeing strange phenomena in the lake. One of the first stories told of a man crossing the lake with his two tethered horses swimming behind. Some strange force pulled the animals under, and the man only saved himself by cutting the horses loose.

Witnesses say the creature is up to 50 feet long, with green skin, several humps, and a huge horse-like head. Some people have managed to view it closely as it ate water vegetation, and they said the Ogopogo had small feet or fins. It could be the North American cousin of the Loch Ness Monster. Most sightings have come from around the city of Kelowna, near the center of the lake, and many monster watchers now agree that it seems to live in the area originally indicated in native legend.

SPOTLIGHT ON...CRYPTOZOOLOGY

Cryptozoology is the study of animals that haven't been proven to exist. It also includes extinct animals, such as dinosaurs, as well as beasts that are considered mythological, like the Ogopogo or the Loch Ness Monster. In other words, there is an entire field of study based on things that, well, don't exist. Except when they do: The Okapi, an animal that looks like a cross between a zebra and a giraffe and the former symbol of the International Society of Cryptozoology, used to be considered a myth—until an Okapi carcass was discovered in 1901.

▶ OUIJA BOARDS ◀

Ouija boards are known to teenagers across the world as the easiest way to create spooky, hair-raising experiences. Most people see them as a toy, something to play with. The fact that they were even mass-produced by toy companies only adds to the harmless fun factor. However, many expert mediums believe they should not be approached with such a nonchalant attitude. They say that countless people end up in dire straits simply from fooling around with Ouija boards, as some have experienced mental breakdowns or disintegrating relationships, others end up possessed by spirits, and some are even driven to suicide.

No one is precisely sure when the first Ouija board was made, but it seems that similar types of apparatus have been around for well over a century. The board itself consists of the letters of the alphabet, the numbers zero to nine, and the words "yes" and "no." (In fact, the name Ouija comes from the words for "yes" in French and German.) The people using the board all gently touch a pointer that slides around the board, forming words that answer the questions asked by the users.

Officially, manufacturers of the boards say the boards work by tapping into the collective subconscious, but the item is generally regarded as a way to talk to spirits. Indeed, sales of the board peaked during World War II as people tried to contact the loved ones they had lost in the course of the conflict. The Ouija board also had a resurgence in the 1960s during a time of heightened spiritual interest. It was marketed as a game, but media stories questioning the effect of the board on people's emotional, spiritual, and psychological equilibrium led to the items being removed from a lot of shops.

There are many potential dangers with the board. If the users are trying to contact the spirit world, then they are probably dealing with something they know nothing about. Some claim that especially mischievous or evil spirits will try to contact people who are using Ouija boards, especially when the users don't have a clear idea of what they are doing. But, like modern technology, viewed and operated in the correct, careful way, the boards can bring a lot of enjoyment.

Experts are particularly keen to warn people of nervous dispositions, who may be susceptible to unhealthy suggestion, to stay

They're doing it wrong.

away from Ouija boards. Users have reported extreme external activity during sessions, with inanimate objects moving independently and lights flicking on and off. There's no definitive account or explanation for what causes the words to be spelled out.

There are some Ouija board experiences that actually prove to be life-changing successes. Many established mediums began their careers using Ouija boards, and there is a strong argument that the boards help you become more sensitive to and appreciative of the spirit world. One such case happened in 1913 to Pearl Curran, a housewife from St. Louis. Curran was dabbling with a friend's board when a spirit supposedly called Patience Worth contacted her. As Curran's relationship with this entity progressed, she started to practice automatic writing, resulting in the production of a multitude of works of poetry, drama, and fiction.

Of course there is always the possibility that Curran was a naturally gifted writer and just pretended a spirit had initiated the writing. She may even have been the unwitting

reincarnation of Patience Worth. In either case, her writing was of high enough quality to be published and receive substantial acclaim from readers.

However, not all experiences have this result. Whatever intellect is being harnessed, the fact is that with Ouija boards, as with life in general, it is best to be careful with things you know little about.

A CASE IN POINT: THE EXORCIST

While Ouija boards have been popular for over a century, many people believe that they're definitely not harmless. Movies have helped contribute to this perception. The most famous is probably *The Exorcist* (1973), about a girl suffering from demonic possession. Early in the film, she plays with a Ouija board, communicating with someone named "Captain Howdy." It's all downhill from there: Her bed shakes, her head spins around, she vomits, she verbally abuses her visitors, and she speaks backward. Not surprisingly, the movie freaked people out, and many went home and burned their Ouija boards.

▶ POLTERGEISTS ◀

In German, the word "poltergeist" means "noisy ghost." It is an apt title since, out of all paranormal occurrences, poltergeists are reported to be the most physical, forceful, and frightening. They are supposed to be capable of making objects fly across the room, shaking furniture, and producing strange, loud noises. They are often believed to be dangerous, and can leave people in a severe state of trauma. The most intriguing aspect of poltergeists is that they appear to be caused by human predicaments and mental powers. In fact, they are such a well-studied phenomenon that science has actually taken an active and interested role in researching them.

Our traditional concept of a ghost or a haunting usually involves the lost soul of a deceased person who is spiritually trapped in the same place where he or she lived or died. It is as if they have not realized their time has passed, and they are not selective about whom they appear to. Indeed, it is generally thought that ghosts do not even realize the modern world is happening around them. Many believe that poltergeists, on the other hand, do interact, disruptively, with their environment. Their disturbances can begin and end abruptly, and they appear to have an intrusive relationship with the people close by. Also, unlike traditional hauntings, it is believed they actually need a human to be the catalyst, or agent, for their activity.

This agent is crucial for poltergeist occurrences. Indeed, experts believe the agent is actually the root cause. It is understood that any type of person can be an agent, but it is alleged that young women are particularly susceptible to poltergeist activity. Although many agents are said to be stable, balanced individuals with no control over the poltergeist, it is widely recognized that some agents have deep-seated mental difficulties. Extreme states of anxiety, depression, hysteria, anger, schizophrenia, and emotional fatigue all seem to be powerful catalysts for poltergeist activity. Similarly, highly stressed individuals are regularly found to be poltergeist agents. The resulting events only serve to heighten any problems the agent has.

People who report poltergeist disturbances describe the following initial symptoms: Banging or knocking noises, awful smells, inexplicable lights, flying or moving objects, and electrical equipment failures. If the cause is not sorted out as time goes on, the activity becomes more and more extreme. Many experts sincerely believe poltergeists are both psychically and mentally dangerous. They say that a person cannot run or move to escape from the poltergeist, that because the agent is responsible for its disturbances, it follows them. Reports of more advanced poltergeist activity involve random fires igniting, and vague apparitions appearing. Poltergeist activity is typically observed by everyone in the room, and the disturbance involves genuine physical activity, rather than imagined events.

Poltergeists have been studied for decades, and scientists and experts have reached some conclusions. Many believe poltergeists are created by the agent releasing psychokinetic energy in an attempt to relieve stress. Psychokinesis is the idea of "mind over matter," and some experts believe that people expel huge amounts of psychokinetic energy when under pressure. The actual activity caused by the poltergeist that occurs is also symbolic of the problem. So for example, some agents who feel intense guilt might inspire a poltergeist to physically beat them, and end up bruised all over. If an agent is incredibly angry with someone, then that person's property may be thrown across the room and smashed by psychokinetic power. In almost all cases, the agents appear to be as scared as everyone else, and do not realize that they are causing these events.

Experts agree that poltergeist activity is possible to solve, and many strongly suggest that those who experience it should seek help immediately. Whether the help comes from a priest or a psychologist, it seems clear that poltergeist agents have an incredible power running loose that needs to be tamed. Once the cause is addressed, or even when the agent realizes that he or she is the root of the disturbances, the activity often stops. As with many paranormal experiences, the horror of poltergeists is not created by some unseen beast or phantom, but by the inexplicable power of the human mind.

FUN FACTS ABOUT POLTERGEISTS

In 1698 a "Stone-Throwing Devil" haunted a New Hampshire, England, tavern. He did nothing but throw things, including "stones, bricks, brick-bats . . . hammers, mauls, iron-crows, and . . . utensils."

In 1931 a British family was haunted by a poltergeist that turned out to be a talking mongoose named Gef.

In 2011, a lecherous poltergeist groped a British grandmother. A news report called the ghost "rude."

Several actors involved in the *Poltergeist* movies died under mysterious circumstances.

In 1991, a New York man sued his house's former owner for not revealing that the house was haunted before she sold it to him. He won.

► THE QUEEN OF SHEBA ◄

The mystical figure known as the Queen of Sheba is recorded in the First Book of Kings in the Old Testament. It states that around the tenth century BCE a queen of the rich trading nation of Sheba decided to meet the great King Solomon. She did not believe the stories she had been told of Solomon's wisdom, and brought many difficult questions to test him. When his replies met with her approval, she gave him plentiful gifts of gold, spices, and precious stones. In return, Solomon gave the queen "all her desire," and after their meeting she returned to her own country. The story is repeated in the second Book of Chronicles. Even Jesus spoke of a queen of the south who came to hear the wisdom of Solomon. Other than this, precious few pieces of historical evidence have survived, but that has not stopped the growth of countless myths and stories. So who was the real Queen of Sheba?

Perhaps the most famous and important extension of her story is the one connected with Ethiopia. In 1320 an Ethiopian monk named Yetshak wrote a compendium of legends called *Kebra Negast* or *Glory of the Kings*. In it, he said that when the Queen of Sheba, referred to in Ethiopian as *Makeda*, visited Solomon, she was seduced by the great king. Solomon had said that the queen was welcome to his hospitality, but must not take anything without asking. During the night, the Queen suffered a terrible thirst caused by a spicy meal Solomon fed her and she drank the water placed by her bed. The king said she had broken the rules, and must sleep with him as repayment. Nine months later she gave birth to a boy called Menelik.

The much bejeweled Queen of Sheba, here engaged in a ferocious staring contest with the artist.

Who was the real Queen of Sheba?

SPOTLIGHT ON...KING SOLOMON

King Solomon must have been a pretty big deal for the Queen of Sheba to arrive bringing such riches. In fact, the Bible says he was known for his wisdom. In one story, two women came to him with a baby, each claiming to be the baby's mother. To test them, Solomon suggested dividing the baby in half. One woman agreed, the other begged him not to hurt the child. Solomon declared the second woman the real mom, and gave her the child.

Ethiopians believe that the queen and her son both accepted the Jewish faith, and that Menelik founded the Solomon dynasty (both Jewish and Christian) in Aksum, Ethiopia.

At around the time Yetshak was compiling his tome, other legends were forming in Europe. A thirteenth-century story told in the *Legenda Aurea* stated that the queen was a prophetess connected to the crucifixion of Christ. Over time, the idea of the Queen of Sheba also became an integral part of religious decorations and art. She was often seen as a sorceress, and later as a seductress. Strangely, she is also featured as having a secret deformity—French Gothic sculpture often shows her having a webbed foot. The *Temptation of Saint Anthony* by French novelist Gustave Flaubert likewise depicts the queen as a lustful temptress with a withered limb.

This imperfection may have arisen from earlier Jewish and Islamic references. In both the Koran and the Jewish Book called the Targum Sheni, the queen meets Solomon and reveals that she has hairy feet. The Jewish tradition later portrays her as a demon or seductress, whereas Islamic legend states that Solomon used his magicians' power to remove her excess hair, and then married her. Muslims call the Queen of Sheba *Balkis*, and believe that her great nation was based in Yemen. The Koran describes Sheba as composed of two gardens, irrigated by a great dam. Healthy fields and access to waterways imply that the nation was prosperous.

Archaeological proof of this has been uncovered in southern Arabia. The remains of a great dam can be viewed in the Mareb region of Yemen. This dam collapsed in 543 CE, but scientists have deduced that it would have been used to irrigate over 500 acres of farmland. In recent years, archaeologists have finished restoring an ancient temple known as the Throne of Balkis, in the Mareb region. The structure dates from the tenth century BCE, so it is from the era during which we believe the queen lived. Two miles to the east of the Mareb region, another ancient building, known as the Temple of the Moon God, is also being studied. Scientists using radar equipment believe this is an extremely large and elaborate structure, and could yield the answers to many Sheba mysteries. Unfortunately such investigations have been plagued over the years by political indifference and, until these areas become more secure for researchers to study, the true history of Sheba may continue to be obscured by myth and legend.

► THE ROSICRUCIANS ◄

In 1614, a pamphlet called *Fama Fraternitatis Rosae Crucis* was published. It described a secret brotherly order of non-Catholic Christians who were striving for knowledge of alchemy and magic. This group, known as the Rosicrucian Brotherhood, was said to be founded in 1408 by a former monk and nobleman, Christian Rosenkreuz. Rosenkreuz was thought to have traveled through Damascus, Jerusalem, and Fez, and had acquired knowledge of magical Arabian practices and Egyptian spiritualism. The Rosicrucian movement he inspired believed in the ability to make gold, and was devoted to the secret study of nature's mystical properties. The Rosicrucians were said to be concerned with encouraging the enlightenment of mankind, and waiting for the day when it would be free of the shackles of the organized Church.

Entry into the order was said to be a secret process, and only special, chosen individuals would be admitted. The brotherhood's background and direction were confirmed in 1615 with the publication of the *Confessio Fraternitatis*, or "Confession of the Brotherhood," and the "Third Chemical Wedding of Christian Rosenkreuz." These writings generated much interest in the movement, and divisions of the order were instigated throughout Europe. It is generally felt that the Rosicrucians may have been one of the precursors to the Freemason fraternity, but how much reality is behind their mythical heritage?

Some sources suggest there may have been some groups similar to the Rosicrucians dating from around the twelfth century in Europe and Asia. However, the brotherhood detailed in the texts of the 1610s was purely the fictional work of John Valentin Andrea, a Lutherian philosopher and theologian. Andrea admitted to writing the pamphlets as a satire of the prevalent deep interest in mysticism and occultism. By

SPOTLIGHT ON...SECRET SOCIETIES

Freemansons, Rosicrucians, Illuminati—why do secret societies exist? It's difficult to determine their goals, since they keep their practices under wraps. But several brotherhoods do seem to have common characteristics. Here are a few similarities.

- ※ They look for knowledge in nature.
- ※ They believe in universal, hidden truths, inaccessible to the rest of us.
- ※ They often only admit guys (sorry, ladies).
- ※ They take oaths.
- ※ They have their own set of rituals.

combining contemporary tales of knighthood and far-off lands with the romantic notions of the time, many felt that Andrea was trying to promote antipapal, Protestant ideas. Certainly, he denounced the whole issue of Rosicrucians as mere folly for the rest of his life, even though the order's sacred symbol of a rose in the center of a cross was actually taken from Andrea's own family shield. But Andrea's writing started something he never intended: The original satirical works ended up being viewed seriously. In the late seventeenth century, new Rosicrucian groups claiming direct descent from those mentioned in Andrea's writings sprang up across Europe. In the mid-eighteenth century Rosicrucianism apparently helped to establish the Freemasonry movement. It is said that Saint-Germain the Deathless was instrumental in both organizations. (Certainly his claimed abilities in alchemy, medicine, and transmutation would have been of immense interest to the early followers.) The Scottish Masonic movement is believed to have retained many Rosicrucian influences, and in 1866, centers of Masonic Rosicrucianism were created throughout Britain and America.

These Rosicrucian movements have continued to this day largely as a select branch of the Freemason community, and around 1910 Harvey Spencer Lewis founded the Ancient Mystical Order Rosae Crucis, or AMORC, in California. Now generally accepted as being the main worldwide division of the movement, AMORC has followers and lodgers from all over the world. The AMORC headquarters in San Jose is believed to be a massive complex that houses a museum, temple, auditorium, planetarium, art gallery, and library. The group holds most of its practices in utmost secrecy, and entry into the Order is said to be limited to select, high-achieving freemasons. Many conspiracy theorists claim that other Rosicrucian orders try to entice people into their groups through suggestive advertising and false claims.

AMORC's stated aim is to encourage the spiritual liberation of people so that individuals can find their own free versions of God. The original idea of reducing the need for organized, church-based religion still persists. It is believed that Rosicrucian followers also strive for knowledge in the secrets of nature—in the symbolic properties of art, literature, and ancient history—and in the development of man's psychic abilities. Critics of the movement claim that it promotes anti-Christian doctrines. As with many secret organizations, the imaginations of the curious can create theories far more outlandish than the truth. And in this area Rosicrucians are unique, as it seems it was the fiction-driven creative mind of John Andrea that actually started the movement in the first place.

► ROSWELL ◄

Through the hazy black-and-white footage, the relaxed shape of a bloated, swollen-headed, six-fingered humanoid figure can just barely be seen. The grainy scene is a bizarre image of death as the pathologist cuts into the alien skin. Could this be the most incredible evidence ever uncovered to prove that something out of this world really did land at Roswell over 50 years ago?

On July 7, 1947, the wreckage of a strange vehicle and some nonhuman bodies were found on the Foster ranch just outside Roswell. The next day, a press officer from the Roswell Army Air Fields was happy to announce to the *Roswell Daily Record* that the 509th Bomb Group, an elite section of the Air Force, had salvaged an alien vessel. Immediately his words were refuted. The US 8th Air Force's commanding officer, General Roger Ramey, said they had actually recovered an experimental balloon. Ramey's explanation was quickly adopted as the official line throughout the following years, and this technique of outright denial would become common among governments questioned about flying saucer stories.

Although the public initially accepted the official version of events, this episode sparked a consistent stream of UFO sightings, particularly around remote US Air Force bases. Sites such as Area 51 in Nevada, and the government's denial of its existence, led to suspicion and conspiracy theories. The 1947 incident at Roswell itself has also never quite left the public consciousness. In 1994 a New Mexico

The Roswell crash scene...but why was there no debris left after the supposed crash?

congressman instigated an inquiry into the affair. The investigative department of the US Congress, known as the General Accounting Office (GAO), discovered that many relevant US Air Force documents had gone missing or had been destroyed. However, the GAO also came to the conclusion that it was, indeed, a weather balloon that had been recovered from the Foster ranch, and the bodies there were in fact anthropomorphic dummies. Case closed.

Little did US officials realize that the Roswell incident was about to be broadcast across the globe. In 1992, a British media businessman, Ray Santilli, was in Cleveland, Ohio, to meet a retired cameraman. Santilli wanted to buy some vintage 1955 Elvis footage from the man, who revealed he also had some interesting alien autopsy film from his time in the military. Santilli purchased the film in November 1994 and agreed to show it at the British UFO Research Association annual conference on August 19, 1995. However, by March 1995 news of the film had been released to the media, and an official world premiere of the footage was needed. It took place in front of invited guests at the Museum of London on May 5. By the end of August 1995, millions of people around the world had seen film of a supposed alien autopsy.

Although this was compelling evidence, doubters immediately began voicing their theories about the film. The most obvious suspicion was that the autopsy had been created using theatrical special effects. Many experts believe the film is fake, but they also believe it is of very high quality. The Hollywood effects industry is a hard world to break into—insiders have friends and contacts across a wide range of companies—but so far no one within that industry has been identified as the creator of the

Roswell film. Other experts in the field of biology are less convinced that the body is entirely man-made, and some suspect that it may be a human being adapted to look otherworldly.

There are many more questions about the Roswell autopsy. The cameraman's identity is not known, although a bizarre film was released where someone purporting to be the cameraman attempted to explain his involvement. Santilli has never released the footage he has of another alien autopsy and has never really allowed any of his films to be subjected to proper scrutiny. Most importantly, the aliens in the footage look nothing like the bodies witnesses saw recovered from the New Mexico desert floor. All experts who view the autopsy film agree that it is a fake. Santilli has made a great deal of money from the Roswell autopsy footage, and he still maintains that it is genuine. The rest of us will probably never know. The public's natural instinct is to question governmental denials, but the other options here are also so unreliable that it's very hard to believe otherwise.

► SÉANCES ◄

Séances are an age-old way for the living to attempt communication with the dead. The popular image of a group sitting around a table, holding hands, with the room lights flickering is a little overdramatic, but not so far from the truth. Many people believe the collective energy of a number of participants, or "sitters," helps to attract spirits. Generally, there should also be an experienced medium who channels the messages and helps control the sitting. Although séances and séance mediums had a reputation for trickery and fraudulent practices in the past, many today think they provide an interesting way to explore the world of spirits and the past.

People who hold séances recommend the following guidelines: Before a séance can begin, it is necessary to have a particular spirit in mind. It also helps if a relative, or someone who knew the spirit in their lifetime, is part of the group—this is a reason why attempts to contact the ghosts of Elvis and other well-known people tend to be unsuccessful. Mediums say that the spirit in question will often know that the séance is going to happen, and will want to talk. The room should be a peaceful environment, and the sitters must be comfortable and undisturbed. They should sit in a circle, or around a table, and may hold hands if they wish, although that is not essential. Together, they mentally call the spirit they are searching for.

Often the medium enters a trance-like state and will allegedly begin channeling messages from the spirit world. Sometimes this coincides with odd physical experiences, such as a cool breeze wafting through, strange scents of perfumes, or a tickling sensation on the skin. Often, sitters also report feeling a slight pain corresponding to how

DID YOU KNOW...HOUDINI STILL HASN'T PERFORMED HIS LAST STUNT?

Though magician and escape artist Harry Houdini died in 1926, fans are still waiting for him to pull off his greatest trick. He and his wife agreed that after he died she would try to contact his spirit every year on the anniversary of his death—Halloween. She held the annual séance for ten years, but Houdini never answered. In the late 1930s, one of Houdini's fans took over and has been holding the event ever since.

A séance in progress.

the spirit died—for example, a chest pain is felt with a spirit who died of a heart attack. Ideally, the medium finds the spirit the sitters have asked for, but it is said that sometimes other spirits are also eager to chat. The medium leads the discussion, and allows it to continue for as long as the sitters want.

With a professional psychic, the chances of having a bad experience are said to be very slim, and many people feel that a séance can act as a significant healing process for both the bereaved and the deceased.

► THE SHROUD OF TURIN ◄

The Shroud of Turin is probably the most famous religious relic in the world. The cloth measures thirteen-and-a-half feet long by four-and-a-half feet wide, and clearly depicts the body of a bearded man, said to be Jesus Christ. Its legend states that it was used by Joseph of Arimathea to wrap the body of Christ after his crucifixion. Its first appearance in recorded history was in 1357, in the little village of Lirey, in France. In 1457 it was taken to Chambéry, in the Savoy region of the country, and in 1532 the shroud was almost destroyed in a fierce fire. This experience left charred marks on the corner of the folds in the fabric, and in 1578 it was taken to Turin where it has remained ever since. The Catholic Church is convinced that the shroud genuinely possesses a physical record of Christ's body, and the cloth is now only shown to the public on rare occasions.

In 1389, the Bishop of Troyes (where the village of Lirey was located) asked Pope Clement VII to publicly rule that the shroud was merely a painting. He stated that the image had actually been painted by an artist, originally as decoration, but the priests in Lirey had started duping the local public into believing it was Christ's authentic death shroud. The Pope bowed to the bishop's wishes, but was hardly resolute. He declared that the shroud could keep being exhibited, but each time it was shown, the local priest had to announce to the assembled public that the relic only depicted a painted copy of Christ's real cloth.

Over the years such practices fell away, and authenticity of the shroud was assumed. The intellectual advances of the Scientific Revolution and the Enlightenment seemed to corroborate this belief. In 1898 photographic experts revealed the image was actually a

I don't know about the other two, but the one on the right is definitely not Jesus.

negative picture, and seen in reverse tones, the outline showed a much more detailed view of the body. By 1901, Dr. Paul Vignon produced a theory that such a phenomenon was caused by ammonia emanating from Christ's dead body after his terrible death. Vignon believed the resulting image was therefore beyond the ability of any forger, and must have been authentic.

But more recent studies have determined otherwise. In 1979 Dr. Walter McCrone conducted a series of advanced scientific tests on samples of the shroud. Using microscopic and microchemical forensic techniques, McCrone and his associates discovered particles of red ochre and vermilion pigment mixed with a tempera medium. No blood was found on the cloth. Tempera was a substance widely used by medieval painters, and recent theories suggest that the original light yellow paint has turned dark brown over the centuries. Similarly, the background cloth has actually faded to a paler hue, thus causing the strange negative image effect, misunderstood by earlier researchers.

In 1988, laboratories in America, Switzerland, and England performed examinations on sections of the cloth. All three concluded the material was produced between 1260 and 1390. Supporting evidence also indicates that the shroud may not be authentic. The Greek New Testament claims Christ was actually wrapped in strips of linen, rather than a whole sheet of cloth. We also have no idea of the shroud's location or origin before the fourteenth century.

Despite these questions surrounding the shroud, some investigators continue to search for proof of its authenticity. One recent theory states that the samples taken for carbon dating were contaminated by fungi and bacteria that had grown in the cloth over the centuries. This idea also explains some dressings on Egyptian mummies that have been carbon dated at an age many hundreds of years later than the remains they cover. And so, despite the ongoing efforts of scientists, the legend and mystery of the Shroud of Turin endures.

A CASE IN POINT: VERONICA'S VEIL

The Veil of Veronica is another holy relic that people say bears the image of Christ. Legend says a woman named Veronica used her veil to wipe Jesus's face as he carried his cross to Calvary. Supposedly the Vatican recovered the veil and displayed it annually. However, in 1999, a scholar found the "real" veil in an Italian abby. That veil depicts a bearded man with long hair and red, bloodlike droplets. Skeptics believe the cloth is an attempt to copy the shroud.

SPONTANEOUS HUMAN COMBUSTION

The mere notion that a human being has the potential to burst into flames without the help of an external ignition source seems too ridiculous for study. Surely there is nothing inside the body that could create such a reaction? And yet, for over three hundred years, records have testified to a phenomenon where people, with no prior warning or exposure to naked flames, simply combust in a fit of intense heat. In most reported cases, all that is left is a pile of ash and perhaps a random charred limb. The fact that no damage ever seems to be done to nearby textiles leaves experts perplexed. This inexplicable phenomenon is called spontaneous human combustion.

Many of those who are supposed to have suffered from spontaneous human combustion, or SHC, were often simply sitting in a chair when the event affected them. At one time, it was thought many subjects were alcoholics, and that the spontaneous human combustion was caused by a chemical reaction brought on by alcohol in the blood and a fit of geriatric frustration. This is now largely discredited, but there are some common qualities in occurrences of SHC.

The actual damage to the bodies affected by SHC appears to be created by a heat more intense than even that of a crematorium. A universal quality of spontaneous human combustion occurrences is that despite this extreme temperature—which experts believe is probably around 1112°F—objects or material around the person do not appear to be destroyed, although obviously their clothing is burnt, and sometimes there is a patch of scorched carpet where their feet would have been. In one reported case, a woman died following an incidence of SHC in bed and the sheets were not even marked. However, occasionally a greasy, sooty dust is found on ceilings and walls nearby.

In 1673 the Frenchman James Dupont provided a fairly comprehensive examination of the phenomenon and its many recorded cases in his book *De Incendiis Corporis Humani Spontaneis*. Dupont's interest in the subject was initially aroused by the Nicolle Millet court case. In this instance, a man was found not guilty of murdering his wife, Nicolle, because the jury ruled that she had actually suffered an attack of spontaneous human combustion. From the late-seventeenth

A similar event occurred in France, when on November 17, 1998, the few remains of a 67-year-old woman called Gisele were found in her farmhouse near Honfleur. Only a pile of ashes and her left foot—with slipper still on—were reportedly discovered. In this case, even the wheelchair she was sitting in had disintegrated, although the rest of her farmhouse did not appear to have been affected.

In such cases, police investigators can only take a guess or choose the most plausible option given the seemingly inconsistent facts. Spontaneous human combustion investigators themselves have no satisfactory explanations. The supposedly potent mixture of anger and alcohol has no scientific basis. The suggestion that the phenomenon is caused by excessive fat deposits that catch fire has also been dismissed, while the idea that it is caused by some error in the body's electrical system is unverifiable.

century, the idea of SHC gained credence and acceptance in popular life. Indeed, Charles Dickens used the phenomenon as the reason of death for a character called Krook in his 1852 novel, *Bleak House*.

The most celebrated case of SHC allegedly happened on July 2, 1951, to a 67-year-old pensioner from Florida named Mary Reeser. The only parts of Reeser's body to be found were her skull, which had shrunk to the size of a baseball, her spinal column, her left foot, and a pile of ash still in her armchair. The authorities declared she had died in a normal household fire, but no part of her apartment, including cotton sheets and a pile of newspapers left nearby, was said to be damaged.

After all of the other options have been considered and dismissed, we may have to just throw up our hands and call it an "act of God"—that's about as good an answer as we can provide for this truly inexplicable mystery. But in the meantime, it's always worth paying attention to a skyrocketing temperature.

▶ STIGMATA ◀

Stigmata have been such well-documented, historical phenomena that many skeptics have come to accept their legitimacy. The affliction creates marks on the body's hands, feet, sides, and brow which are believed to reflect the wounds Christ suffered on the cross. The marks often bleed or secrete a liquid, and can appear and disappear in a matter of hours. Most reported cases of stigmata have typically been saints, or the devoutly religious. Many believe that the phenomenon leaves a physical representation of Christ's wounds and stigmatics often feel pain near the marks, and many report a lifelong sense of despair and suffering. Some even say they feel the lashing of whips across their backs. Religious followers believe that the pain is an integral part of stigmata.

The first celebrated stigmatic was Saint Francis of Assisi. His holy marks appeared in 1222 and were of an extent never subsequently equaled. It is said that the skin on his hands and feet actually grew out of the wounds to form calluses in the shape of nails. Since his time, there have been over three hundred reported stigmatics, 62 of which were saints. Georgio Bongiavani is one of the most well-known recent stigmatics in recent memory. In his case, wounds on his hands and forehead seemed to have appeared and disappeared almost at will. But the explanation for stigmata is still a mystery. Doctors have reported cases in which the blood secreted by the wounds was of a different type than the stigmatic's own blood. Wounds have also secreted an unknown liquid, and some have even exuded a perfume.

One popular theory states that stigmata are psychosomatic afflictions brought on by extreme levels of worship. Some believe

A CASE IN POINT: PADRE PIO

An Italian monk called Padre Pio experienced the stigmata on his hands, feet, and side for over 50 years. There are numerous photographs of the wounds bleeding, though he often kept them covered with bandages. Several doctors studied the wounds but could not explain their occurrence, and they were never infected. The wounds reportedly disappeared hours before he died, in 1968.

stigmatics unconsciously bring about these wounds though their devotion to Christ. Many stigmatics have reported their wounds appearing in greatest intensity around the holy days of Easter, when the sufferers are most engaged in religious events. Similarly, each stigmatic's wounds generally correspond to the marks on the statue of the person they most often worship. If the statue is nailed through the wrist and ankles, their wounds appear in the wrist and ankles. But of course, there is another theory: that stigmata are sent by God as a gift to only the most holy.

Padre Pio in action.

▶ STONEHENGE ◀

Stonehenge is a standing rock formation that lies on Salisbury Plain in the county of Wiltshire, England. The whole area is regarded as mystical, and is also believed to be the center of the crop circle phenomenon. Stonehenge itself was constructed in three stages. The first stage began in about 3,000 BCE, when a circular ditch was dug around the site, forming a raised bank two yards high and 106 yards in diameter. Inside the bank, 56 shallow holes were dug and refilled, and the first rock, the Heel Stone, was introduced, positioned to mark the axis of sunrise at the summer solstice. Two smaller entrance stones were put in place, then 40 wooden posts, marking positions of the sun, were erected.

Around 2,000 BCE, a two-mile avenue to the River Avon was created. From southwest Wales, the builders imported 82 bluestones, weighing over four tons each. To reach the site, they would have had to travel 240 miles over land and water. These bluestones formed a double circle inside the site. Some believe the builders never finished this design because they already intended to erect the third, and most impressive, phase.

This began around 1900 BCE, with the selection of 75 loose blocks of sandstone, known

Despite common thinking, Stonehenge predates the Druids by almost two thousand years.

as sarsens, from Avebury, 20 miles away. These 27-ton, 17-foot-long rocks were pulled to the site using rollers and ropes, then shaped and lifted into upright positions. The architectural detail here is remarkable, and the lintel stones that cap the pillars are actually curved to fit in the large circle. The Welsh bluestones were then repositioned, completing the structure.

The stones were placed at specific points demonstrating the position of the sun and moon at important times. The site was used continually until about 1,000 BCE, but we still do not know exactly what it was used for. Very little human or cultural debris has been found on the site, so there are no definitive answers.

Some experts say that this absence of historic litter suggests that the structure was a temple or sacred site. Many of the other 900 stone circles in Britain served many uses and were often meeting places, so they often have remnants of ancient day-to-day life. Similarly, the sheer scale of the project indicates that Stonehenge was immensely important. The bluestones brought from Wales were exceedingly valuable to the ancient Britons, and were ideal for a temple.

FUN FACTS ABOUT...STONEHENGE

* Stonehenge was always a major tourist attraction. Evidence from nearby graves shows that people visited from miles away.
* Stonehenge was better than the doctor. So many people buried nearby had medical problems that it may have been a place of healing, like an ancient Lourdes.
* Stonehenge draws more hippies than Woodstock. From 1972 to 1985, the Stonehenge Free Festival attracted counterculture groups such as the Tepee People and the New Age Travellers.
* Stonehenge can be dangerous. At a riot called the Battle of the Beanfield, police brutally attacked festival-goers. The site, however, only drew more visitors after that.

Stonehenge also may have been used as a burial site. Excavators have discovered that the 56 shallow holes from the first phase contained cremated bones. There are also barrows, or burial tombs, of later Bronze Age warriors around the outlying area.

Because of Stonehenge's apparent connection to important astronomical events, a host of other theories have arisen. It may have been used as an observatory, or even a lunar calendar. In 1965, Gerald S. Hawkins,

One of those stones looks eerily human, right?

an astronomer at Boston University, published a book entitled *Stonehenge Uncoded*, which claimed that a computer had proven that Stonehenge marked many astronomical alignments. Hawkins even wrote that Stonehenge was a computer itself, designed by the ancient Britons to read the stars and calculate upcoming eclipses. However, many experts are skeptical about these claims.

In the seventeenth century, historians believed the structure had been built by ancient Celtic priests, and many modern druids today feel it is their right to perform rituals and ceremonies at the site. But they are no longer allowed to, because damage was occurring to the area. Further, modern druids have no connection to their Celtic namesakes, and Stonehenge was built over 1,000 years before the Celtic druids existed.

In the last few hundred years, many of the stones have been stolen, lost, or collapsed, and poor restoration work has been performed on some of the stones that remain. But interest in the design and the mysterious site itself continues. One legend says that Merlin, the most famous of all Britain's magicians, summoned the stones and set them in place. It is a story in keeping with the mystical tradition of the area. Maybe modern minds just haven't gotten there.

▶ UFO CRASHES ◀

In 1963, a scientist known as Fritz Werner was working on nuclear tests in Arizona. In May of that year, Werner was asked to go on a special assignment—he was flown to Phoenix, and then taken by bus with a group of other men to a destination northwest of the city. The men were told not to talk to each other, and when they unloaded from the vehicle they were shown a crash site. Werner claims that he saw a 30-foot-wide metal disc protruding from the desert sand. He was asked to calculate the speed of the impact, and says that during his time on site he also saw the body of a four-foot-tall creature wearing a silver suit in the medical tent. He was taken back to Arizona and made to sign a nondisclosure agreement.

In 1957, a crashed UFO actually produced physical evidence. On September 18 a journalist named Ibrahim Sued, who worked at a major Brazilian paper called *O Globo*, received a very odd letter. It was unsigned, but said that it was written by a man who saw, while fishing near the town of Ubatuba in Sao Paulo, an odd flying disc almost crash

Evidence of a UFO? Or evidence of shoddy camera work?

into the sea. The anonymous man said the craft was traveling at incredible speeds, and although it missed the water, it exploded in mid-air. The man managed to collect fragments from the strange vessel, which he included in the letter. These pieces were sent for official testing, and the Brazilian agricultural ministry declared the substance was a form of unusually pure magnesium.

CHRONOLOGY: UFO CRASHES

Here are some other famous crash reports—but were they real, or the results of various hoaxes?

- ☀ 1897, Aurora, Texas: A ship with hieroglyphic symbols crashes into a windmill.
- ☀ 1947, Roswell, New Mexico: The Air Force recovers a UFO, but says later that it was just an air balloon.
- ☀ 1952, Flatwoods, Virginia: Townspeople see a ball of fire crash to the earth, and a creature with glowing eyes.
- ☀ 1962, Las Vegas, Nevada: A UFO seen by over a thousand people goes down over an Air Force Base. All the lights in the town go out.
- ☀ 1974, near Chihuahua, Mexico: A UFO collides with a plane.

The Brazilian army and navy also performed experiments, but kept the results secret.

Unlike in more remote areas, UFO researchers have a great advantage when investigating odd incidents in America: There are often plenty of witnesses. On December 9, 1965, hundreds of people saw a bizarre object streaking across the skies over Ohio and Pennsylvania. Some of the airline pilots who witnessed the object felt their planes shake from the turbulence. For six minutes, people watched what they thought was a meteorite travel from northwest to southeast before it seemed to explode. In fact, the object crashed in a wooded area in the town of Kecksberg, and started a small fire. A specialist military team immediately descended on the area, and turned away local police and fire authorities. Witnesses said they had seen the armed unit load a rounded metallic object onto a flatbed truck and cover it in tarpaulin to disguise its load.

One of the most unsettling UFO crashes is reported to have occurred in northern Mexico, in the state of Chihuahua. UFO investigators have obtained documents they say reveal that two US Air Defense radars tracked an unidentified object on August 25, 1974. The object seemed to be entering the atmosphere from orbit, and was heading

UFOs: The future of frisbees.

seemed to have been involved. When they transmitted a message that claimed the second appeared to be metallic and circular in shape, all broadcasts were ordered to stop.

UFO enthusiasts believe the US government heard these messages and immediately organized a response team. The government strongly urged Mexico to accept its help, and when the local authorities ignored the offer, it became involved anyway. Mexican salvage squads had already loaded the two crafts on to a truck and were heading south. By the time the US forces, traveling in helicopters, caught up with them, a terrible tragedy had occurred. All the people with the convoy had somehow been mysteriously killed, so the American team, wearing protective clothing, took charge of the suspect air vehicle. They ferried it slung underneath a cargo helicopter, and took it to a secret installation in the United States.

There is no absolute proof of UFO activity, but investigators claim that more and more official evidence is being revealed to support these stories. The truth may not be "out there," but it could lie hidden in the secret vaults of a government agency.

toward the United States, but veered off at the last minute and disappeared from sight over Mexico. At the same time, Mexican authorities reported that a light airplane had been lost over the area. The next day, Mexican search-and-rescue teams hunting for the downed plane reported that they had found the crash site, and that two aircraft

► VOODOO ◄

Symbols such as pin dolls and skeleton-painted priests are inextricably linked with the popular perception of Voodoo. A combination of Hollywood movies, fictional novels, and comic books have helped instill the idea that Voodoo is a mysterious, evil religion. Many people believe it has been used to bring about the early deaths of unwelcome researchers and to resurrect the zombified bodies of dead believers.

However, those who practice Voodoo say these rumors and myths are borne out of ignorance and misplaced fear. Voodoo, they say, is actually a peaceful religion very similar to the Catholic faith.

Voodoo, also known as *Vodun, Vodoun, Voudou*, or *Sevi Lua*, originated in the West African countries of Nigeria, Benin, and Togo. "Voodoo" is an ancient African word that means "Great Spirit", and the religion likely stretches back many thousands of years. Europeans first heard of Voodoo when slave traders began capturing African workers in the sixteenth century, and deporting them to the West Indies. On arriving in the islands, the slaves were forcibly converted to the Catholic faith, but as there were few outlets for them to actually practice this new religion, many slipped back into their native traditions.

Their religion was founded on the idea of one supreme God—an unknowable but almighty

The spider model, which is commonly used in Voodoo ceremonies, is the second most frightening thing in this photo.

force. Under him lies a network of *Loa*, or spirits, which are broadly equivalent to the Christian idea of patron saints. Each Loa represents a different area of life and has certain qualities. For example, if a farmer was worried about his crops, he might focus his worship on the Loa known as Zaka, the spirit of agriculture. Despite the similarity between these African faiths and their own, the French and Spanish conquerors refused to accept that these enslaved people could have a legitimate religion of their own. The European settlers banned Voodoo, fearing that their slaves were actually worshipping the devil, and slave leaders and priests were beaten into confessing that their rituals were evil.

However, the Voodoo faith continued in secret, particularly in Haiti. Over time it even adopted some aspects of the Catholic religion, as descendants of the original slaves spread throughout the Caribbean. The beliefs of West Indian workers mixed with the Voodoo practices of slaves taken to the American South, and New Orleans, with its fertile blend of French, Spanish, and African cultures, soon became the hub of the new faith. Today, 15 percent of New Orleans citizens, and 60 million people worldwide, practice Voodoo. In 1996 it was also made the official faith of Benin, a small country in West

SPOTLIGHT ON...VOODOO DOLLS

They're not just for revenge anymore. Several ancient cultures have used dolls and effigies in rituals and customs. They've been used for healing, for teaching, during burial, in folk magic, and as talismans. Voodoo dolls are said to serve a similar purpose, in a form of ritual magic called gris gris, which can be used for things such as love, power, luck, healing, finances, and spiritual guidance. Though they can be used for revenge and are most commonly depicted that way, most who practice Voodoo shun that method, sticking to the good stuff.

Africa. Despite this official recognition, there is still a great deal of mystery and fear attached to Voodoo rituals.

The Voodoo temple is called a *Hounfour*, and the leader of the Voodoo ceremony is a male priest called *a Houngan*, or a female priest called a *Mambo*. At the center of the temple there is a post used to contact spirits, and a highly decorated altar. There is a feast before each ceremony, and a particular pattern relating to the Loa being worshipped is outlined on the temple floor. Dancing and chanting accompanied by beats from rattles and religious drums called *Tamboulas* begins the event. One of the dancers, said to be possessed by the Loa, enters a trance and behaves just as the Loa would. An animal, normally a chicken, goat, sheep, or dog, is sacrificed and its blood is collected. This is used to sate the hunger of the Loa.

Although these rites and rituals are used for benevolent purposes—asking for guidance and help—there are also some less savory practices. Voodoo black magic is performed by *Caplatas* or *Bokors* who place curses and stick pins in Voodoo dolls to cause people pain and suffering. But although it's been made famous through appearances in film, television, and bestselling books, this use of Voodoo is rare. In general, the faith is promoted by its followers as a wonderful way to understand the human condition and the world around us. Even though some of the practices might seem a little strange, are they really much different from certain evangelist rituals or Catholic rites? As with many of humanity's mysteries, a little tolerance and understanding goes a long way toward revealing the truth.

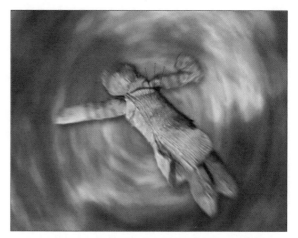

A doll used in the African/West Indian practice of Voodoo

▶ WEEPING STATUES ◀

The phenomenon of weeping or crying religious statues is one of the oldest and most stereotypical images of holy powers in Catholicism. Ireland, South America, and southern Europe all have well-documented accounts of Virgin Mary figurines seeping strange liquids. And, while skeptics may doubt the validity of such occurrences, they are truly miraculous to the local populations.

In November 1992, a six-inch-high, blue-and-white porcelain statue of the Virgin Mary began weeping blood in Santiago, Chile. The figurine, which belonged to a local housewife, became an attraction for local people in the La Cisterna district and was even tested by Chilean police. Doctors at the Santiago coroner's office discovered that the liquid produced by the statue's eyes was human blood.

A similar event happened in the small village of Mura, 35 miles north of Barcelona in Spain. Outside the village church a two-foot-high marble statue of the Virgin Mary had been set on a seven-foot-high pedestal. In March 1998, the local priest, Luis Costa, discovered it was crying tears of blood. Mura residents were convinced the phenomenon was genuine. The statue had not been tampered with, and further investigation revealed the blood was emanating from the figure in a particularly human way.

Even this statue can't resist the emotional power of Leonardo di Caprio's performance in *Titanic*.

Skeptics are quick to dismiss such stories. Some promote fanciful theories that water is soaked up by the base of the statues, mixes with red clay inside them, and then appears through the head as blood. Others are convinced these instances have been created through the use of a simple magic trick. Certainly, it is true that people are rarely around to witness the actual moment when blood appears on such statues. By diverting people's attention, it would be easy to interfere with the figurines unnoticed. But these explanations fail to alter the effect of the phenomenon on a credulous public. Although it is important to discover the truth, this type of religious mysticism is a pleasant way to remind us that there are still some things in life that we just can't explain.

DID YOU KNOW...MOST WEEPING STATUES ARE CONSIDERED HOAXES?

You're shocked; we know. Although the Catholic Church investigates many instances of weeping statues, only a very small number of them are considered valid or are still unverified. In most cases, the liquid secreted by the statues turns out to be paint, water, synthetic liquid, even Mazola oil. The only instance officially recognized by the Vatican is Our Lady of Akita, in Japan, in which a Virgin Mary statue wept over a hundred times and bled from its right hand. Testing suggested that the statue somehow secreted real human blood, tears, and sweat.

► YETI ◄

In 1921, Lieutenant Colonel Charles Kenneth Howard-Bury, a British soldier who had led an expedition up Mount Everest, recounted a puzzling story. His team had been scaling the mountain's north face when they noticed dark shapes moving about in the snow above them. By the time the explorers reached the site, the only signs of life were large, unusual, human-like footprints. Howard-Bury said the Sherpa guides called this creature the *Metoh-Kangmi*. Translated, this became the "Abominable Snowman."

Metoh-Kangmi was a collective term for any of three mythical mountain creatures. Individually, they had their own names: The "Dzu Teh," a large, hairy beast that experts believe is actually one of the rare bear species in the region; "Thelma," which is regarded as being a species of gibbon; and the "Meh-Teh" or "Yeh-Teh," the "man-beast" or "rock dweller." This animal, the "Yeh-Teh," is the most mysterious. It is described as being between five and six feet tall, with reddish hair, long hanging arms, a conical, pointed head, and a human face. This Yeh-Teh is what we now know as the Yeti.

In 1925, N. A. Tombazi, a Greek photographer, was on expedition in the Himalayas when one of the Sherpa guides noticed a figure in the distance. The creature stood upright, just like a human, and was pulling at some rhododendron bushes. The beast

Just think how annoying it would be to live beneath a Yeti. "Stop clomping around up there, you jerk!"

disappeared before Tombazi could capture it on film, but the party headed over to the area where it had been seen and found footprints strangely similar those of humans. There were many more reports of odd tracks in the snow in the following years.

In 1951 the eminent mountaineers Eric Shipton and Michael Ward were part of the Everest Reconnaissance Expedition. They were trying to plot the best route up the mountain when they came upon a set of fresh and unusual footprints. Shipton and Ward took photographs of the thirteen-by-eighteen-inch prints, and followed the trail they made before it eventually disappeared. Sir Edmund Hillary and Sherpa Tenzing Norgay, Everest's two most celebrated visitors, actually found

giant footprints on their way to the summit in 1953. This was particularly interesting because it was supposed that Norgay's father had encountered a Yeti shortly before he died, and Hillary would later lead an effort to find evidence of the Yeti's existence.

When Hillary's 1960 Yeti expedition found nothing, he stated that the beast was nothing more than a fairy tale. But many experts felt Hillary had rushed to his conclusion. Even Hillary's colleague on the mission, Desmond Doig, said the expedition had been too bulky and clumsy. Doig agreed that they had not encountered a Yeti, but neither had they seen a snow leopard, which undoubtedly exists.

This failed expedition killed off much interest in the Yeti, but over the years more unusual footprints were found. In 1974 one of the creatures reportedly attacked a Sherpa girl and her yaks, killing a couple of her animals. In March 1986, Tony Woodbridge, a British physicist doing a sponsored solo run around the Himalayas, had a remarkable face-to-face meeting with the monster. Woodbridge had seen tracks earlier in the day, but thought no more about it until he heard a crashing sound like an avalanche.

Snow had indeed fallen further up the trail, creating a giant, impenetrable frozen wall. Strangely, it looked as if something had slid

DID YOU KNOW...
THE YETI IS A WORLD TRAVELER?

In 2011, Russian researchers said they had found proof of the Yeti in Siberia. They said they found a cave where the Yeti lived, including his sleeping area. They also found footprints in the snow and strands of gray hair, and were 95 percent sure the Yeti was real. The researchers didn't actually see the Yeti, though. Strangely, they didn't try to film the creature, and they didn't hang around waiting for it to come back. (Hey, no one said they were stupid.)

down the snow. Woodbridge followed prints at the bottom of the mound, and just under 500 feet away he spotted a large, hairy, powerfully built creature standing still. The beast did not move an inch, and Woodbridge was lucky enough to have his camera on him. Unfortunately, despite Woodbridge's initial strong convictions, close examinations of his photographs instilled some doubt and a return to the area convinced Woodbridge that he had only encountered a tree stump.

Even if episodes like this do nothing to convince skeptics, many experts agree that the idea of an unknown species of ape is not so far-fetched. Some species of wild cattle and jungle deer have been discovered only in the last ten years. It is possible that undiscovered Yeti-like creatures that have descended from prehistoric apes could be roaming parts of the world. Whatever the scientists and experts prove, Sherpas have already accepted the belief that, in their mountains, they are not alone.

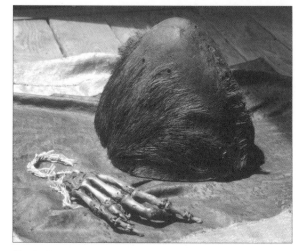

Physical evidence of the Yeti: scalp, hide, and hand.

► ZOMBIES ◄

Much like vampires, zombies are understood as being "undead" – meaning that they've died but can come back, move around, and cause harm to others. But despite the current popularity of movies like *28 Days Later* and TV shows like *Walking Dead*, stories of people being raised from the dead have been around for literally thousands of years. *The Epic of Gilgamesh*—a truly ancient piece of literature—makes reference to this idea, and of course the Bible also has many references to people who have come back to life or who have been raised from the dead.

The idea of zombies is more specific, and developed much later on, but it's still interesting that folklore from such diverse places as medieval Scandinavia, ancient China, and modern Europe all include stories of corpses that can somehow walk around—often controlled by witchcraft. People generally believed that these creatures had come back for revenge, or to haunt the living, but in more recent times the idea has evolved, and when we talk about zombies now we understand them as self-willed creatures with no agenda beyond feeding on the closest piece of living flesh. Most people think of zombies as a thrilling but baseless myth—but it was recently discovered that, through the practice of voodoo, a zombie-like state can actually be achieved.

The center of the zombie world is the island of Hispaniola, in the West Indies. Many peasant workers there believe that evil sorcerers called bokors have the power to bring their deceased loved ones back to life as

DID YOU KNOW...
HOW TO PREPARE FOR A
ZOMBIE APOCALYPSE?

If flesh-eating zombies overran the country, would you be ready? According to the Centers for Disease Control, we wouldn't behave very differently from the way we now react to real emergencies. Zombies can carry infectious viruses, so you'll need to evacuate. First, prep your emergency kit. Set aside enough water, food, and supplies to get you to a safe, zombie-proof refuge. Plan a quick escape route and a family meeting spot. Set aside a list of emergency contact numbers. Finally, don't worry—a zombie outbreak isn't that likely. Right?

unthinking puppets. They believe the bokors then use these unfortunates as their slaves. In a development straight out of *Invasion of the Body Snatchers*, some people have reported members or friends who have been turned into zombies—and as a precaution many poor peasant workers now place heavy stone tablets on top of their loved ones' coffins to keep bokors from snatching the bodies.

The reality is truly frightening, although it does not involve otherworldly powers. Psychiatric experts agree that the people identified as zombies by Haitian folk do have problems and suffer from a variety of serious mental health disorders. Some have suggested that the idea of zombies was a way Haitian culture could explain these naturally unwell people. Others think it is something more sinister.

Using a chemical called tetrodotoxin, a nerve agent found in puffer fish, a bokor is believed to afflict a victim with a deep paralysis. The victim's family thinks he or she is dead, and proceeds with burial. The lack of oxygen in the coffin contributes to brain damage. When the bokor comes to steal the body, the victim is revived using a substance called datura stramonium, or "zombie cucumber," which is also a mind-control drug. Other poisons, like that found in a local cane toad, can be extracted and can act as hallucinogens and anesthetics on the unfortunate victims. They can keeps victims in a permanent trance state, appearing impervious to physical pain. This acts as a warning to other islanders to be wary of the power of bokors.

SCHOOL LIFE

97 Things to Do Before You Finish High School
by Steven Jenkins & Erika Stalder

Been There, Survived That
Getting Through Freshman Year of High School
edited by Karen Macklin

Crap
How to Deal With Annoying Teachers, Bosses, Backstabbers,
and Other Stuff that Stinks
by Erin Elisabeth Conley, Karen Macklin, & Jake Miller

The Dictionary of High School B.S.
From Acne to Varsity, All the Funny, Lame,
and Annoying Aspects of High School Life
by Lois Beckwith

Freshman
Tales of 9th Grade Obsessions, Revelations, and Other Nonsense
by Corinne Mucha

Take Me With You
Off-to-College Advice From One Chick to Another
by Nikki Roddy

Uncool
A Girl's Guide to *Misfitting In*
by Erin Elisabeth Conley

POP CULTURE

The End
50 Apocalyptic Visions From Pop Culture
That You Should Know About...before it's too late
by Laura Barcella

How to Fight, Lie, and Cry Your Way to Popularity (and a prom date)
Lousy Life Lessons from 50 Teen Movies
by Nikki Roddy

Reel Culture
50 Classic Movies You Should Know About
(So You Can Impress Your Friends)
by Mimi O'Connor

Scandalous!
50 Shocking Events You Should Know About
(So You Can Impress Your Friends)
by Hallie Fryd

DATING + RELATIONSHIPS

Crush
A Girl's Guide to Being Crazy in Love
by Erin Elisabeth Conley

The Date Book
A Girl's Guide to Going Out With Someone New
by Erika Stalder

Dumped
A Girl's Guide to Happiness After Heartbreak
by Erin Elisabeth Conley

Girls Against Girls
Why We Are Mean to Each Other, and How We Can Change
by Bonnie Burton

Kiss
A Girl's Guide to Puckering Up
by Erin Elisabeth Conley

The Mother Daughter Cookbook
Recipes to Nourish Relationships
by Lynette Rohrer Shirk

Queer
The Ultimate LGBT Guide for Teens
by Kathy Belge & Marke Bieschke

Split In Two
Keeping It Together When Your Parents Live Apart
by Karen Buscemi

HEALTH 101

Girl in a Funk
Quick Stress Busters (and Why They Work)
by Tanya Napier & Jenn Kollmer

Sex: A Book for Teens
An Uncensored Guide to Your Body, Sex, and Safety
by Nikol Hasler

Skin
The Bare Facts
by Lori Bergamotto

STYLE

The Book of Styling
An Insider's Guide to Creating Your Own Look
by Somer Flaherty

Fashion 101
A Crash Course in Clothing
by Erika Stalder

The Look Book
50 Iconic Beauties and How to Achieve Their Signature Styles
by Erika Stalder

HOW-TO

47 Things You Can Do for the Environment
by Lexi Petronis

87 Ways to Throw a Killer Party
by Melissa Daly

Don't Sit on the Baby
The Ultimate Guide to Sane, Skilled, and Safe Babysitting
by Halley Bondy

Girl in a Fix
Quick Beauty Solutions (and Why They Work)
by Somer Flaherty & Jenn Kollmer

Holy Spokes
A Biking Bible for Everyone
by Rob Coppilillo

Indie Girl
From Starting a Band to Launching a Fashion Company, Nine Ways to Turn Your Creative Talent into Reality
by Arne Johnson & Karen Macklin

In the Driver's Seat
A Girl's Guide to Her First Car
by Erika Stalder

Jeaneology
Crafty Ways to Reinvent Your Old Blues
by Nancy Flynn

Junk-Box Jewelry
25 DIY Low Cost (or No Cost) Jewelry Projects
by Sarah Drew

Start It Up
The Complete Teen Business Guide to Turning Your Passions Into Pay
by Kenrya Rankin

Where's My Stuff
The Ultimate Teen Organizing Guide
by Samantha Moss with Lesley Schwartz

TRUE STORIES

Dear Teen Me
Authors Write Letters to Their Teen Selves
edited by Miranda Kenneally & E. Kristin Anderson

Regine's Book
A Teen Girl's Last Words
by Regine Stokke

Zoo Station
The Story of Christiane F.
by Christiane F.